CW00346295

1 MONTH OF
FREE
READING

at
www.ForgottenBooks.com

By purchasing this book you are
eligible for one month membership to
ForgottenBooks.com, giving you
unlimited access to our entire
collection of over 1,000,000 titles via
our web site and mobile apps.

To claim your free month visit:

www.forgottenbooks.com/free953968

ISBN 978-0-260-52567-3
PIBN 10953968

Historic, archived document

Do not assume content reflects current
scientific knowledge, policies, or practices.

United States Department of Agriculture

BUREAU OF ENTOMOLOGY AND PLANT QUARANTINE

SERVICE AND REGULATORY ANNOUNCEMENTS

OCTOBER–DECEMBER 1937

CONTENTS

QUARANTINE AND OTHER OFFICIAL ANNOUNCEMENTS

ANNOUNCEMENTS RELATING TO DUTCH ELM DISEASE QUARANTINE (NO. 71)

MODIFICATION OF DUTCH ELM DISEASE QUARANTINE REGULATIONS

INTRODUCTORY NOTE

The following modification of the Dutch elm disease quarantine regulations adds to the regulated area the towns of Redding and Weston in Fairfield County, Conn.; the township of Alexandria in Hunterdon County. N. J., and the town of Cornwall in Orange County, N. Y. This action was taken on the basis of intensive inspections made throughout the year which disclosed infections in areas contiguous to the present regulated area.

AVERY S. HOYT,
Acting Chief, Bureau of Entomology and Plant Quarantine.

AMENDMENT NO. 3 TO RULES AND REGULATIONS SUPPLEMENTAL TO NOTICE OF QUARANTINE NO. 71

[Approved November 9, 1937; effective November 9, 1937]

Under authority conferred by the Plant Quarantine Act of August 20, 1912 (37 Stat. 315), as amended by the act of Congress approved March 4, 1917 (39 Stat. 1134, 1165), it is ordered that regulation 3 of the rules and regulations supplemental to Notice of Quarantine No. 71, on account of the Dutch elm disease, which were promulgated on February 20, 1935, as amended effective April 1, 1936, and November 9, 1936, be, and the same is hereby, further amended to read as follows:

REGULATION 3. REGULATED AREAS

In accordance with the provisos to Notice of Quarantine No. 71, the Secretary of Agriculture designates as regulated areas for the purpose of these regulations the counties, townships, towns, and cities listed below, including all cities, towns, boroughs, or other political subdivisions within their limits:

Connecticut.—Towns of Darien, Fairfield, Greenwich, New Canaan, Norwalk. Redding, Ridgefield, Stamford, Weston, Westport, and Wilton, in *Fairfield County.*

New Jersey.—Counties of Bergen, Essex, Hudson, Morris, Passaic, Somerset, and Union; all of *Hunterdon County* except the townships of Delaware, Holland, Kingwood, and West Amwell, and the boroughs of Frenchtown, Lambertville, Milford, and Stockton; townships of Hopewell, Princeton, and West Windsor, and the boroughs of Hopewell, Pennington, and Princeton, in *Mercer County;* all of *Middlesex County* except the townships of Cranbury and Monroe, and the boroughs of Helmetta, Jamesburg, and Spotswood; townships of Holmdel, Matawan, Middletown, Raritan, Shrewsbury, and the boroughs of Atlantic Highlands, Eatontown, Fair Haven, Highlands, Keansburg, Keyport, Little Silver, Long Branch, Matawan, Monmouth Beach, Oceanport, Red Bank, Rumson, Sea Bright, Shrewsbury, Union Beach, and West Long Branch, in *Monmouth County;* all of *Sussex County* except the townships of Montague, Sandyston, Stillwater, and Walpack; townships of Allamuchy, Franklin, Frelinghuysen, Independence, Hope, Liberty. Mansfield, Oxford, Washington, and White, and the boroughs of Belvidere, Hackettstown, and Washington, in *Warren County.*

New York.—Counties of Bronx, Kings, Nassau, New York, Queens, Richmond, Rockland, and Westchester: towns of Blooming Grove, Chester, Cornwall, Goshen, Highland, Minisink, Monroe, Tuxedo. Warwick, Wawayanda, and Woodbury, in *Orange County;* towns of Carmel, Phillipstown, Putnam Valley. and South East, in *Putnam County;* town of Huntington, in *Suffolk County.*

This amendment shall be effective on and after November 9, 1937, and shall on that date supersede amendment No. 2 which became effective on November 9, 1936.

Done at the city of Washington this 9th day of November 1937.

Witness my hand and the seal of the United States Department of Agriculture.

M. L. WILSON,
Acting Secretary of Agriculture.

[SEAL]

[The foregoing amendment was sent to all common carriers doing business in or through the States of Connecticut, New York, and New Jersey.]

NOTICE TO GENERAL PUBLIC THROUGH NEWSPAPERS

UNITED STATES DEPARTMENT OF AGRICULTURE,
BUREAU OF ENTOMOLOGY AND PLANT QUARANTINE,
Washington, D. C., November 9, 1937.

Notice is hereby given that the Secretary of Agriculture, under authority conferred on him by the Plant Quarantine Act of August 20, 1912 (37 Stat. 315), as amended, has promulgated amendment No. 3 to the rules and regulations supplemental to Notice of Quarantine No. 71, on account of the Dutch elm disease, effective on and after November 9, 1937. The purpose of the amendment is to add to the regulated area the towns of Redding and Weston in Fairfield County, Conn.; the township of Alexandria in Hunterdon County, N. J.; and the town of Cornwall in Orange County, N. Y., not heretofore included. Copies of the amendment may be obtained from the Bureau of Entomology and Plant Quarantine, United States Department of Agriculture, Washington, D. C.

M. L. WILSON,
Acting Secretary of Agriculture.

[The above notice was published in the following newspapers: The Times, Hartford, Conn., November 18, 1937; the News, Newark, N. J., November 19, 1937; the Times, New York, N. Y., November 19, 1937.]

INSTRUCTIONS TO POSTMASTERS

POST OFFICE DEPARTMENT,
THIRD ASSISTANT POSTMASTER GENERAL,
Washington, November 16, 1937.

Postmaster:

MY DEAR SIR: Your attention is invited to the inclosed copy of the latest revision of Quarantine Order No. 71 of the United States Department of Agriculture, extending the area covered by the Dutch elm disease quarantine, by which you will be governed. See paragraph 1, section 595, Postal Laws and Regulations, and page 19 of the July 1937 Postal Guide, part I.

Very truly yours,

ROY M. NORTH,
Acting Third Assistant Postmaster General.

ANNOUNCEMENT RELATING TO FRUIT AND VEGETABLE QUARANTINE (NO. 56)

INSTRUCTIONS TO COLLECTORS OF CUSTOMS

QUARANTINE REGULATIONS AFFECTING THE IMPORTATION INTO THE UNITED STATES AND THE INTERSTATE SHIPMENT FROM HAWAII AND PUERTO RICO OF FROZEN FRUITS, ISSUED BY THE SECRETARY OF AGRICULTURE, UNDER THE AUTHORITY OF PLANT QUARANTINES 13, 56, AND 58 (T. D. 49247)

TREASURY DEPARTMENT,
OFFICE OF THE COMMISSIONER OF CUSTOMS,
Washington, D. C., November 8, 1937.

To Collectors of Customs and Others Concerned:

Plant Quarantine circulars 462, 463, and 464 making provision for the importation into the United States and the interstate shipment from Hawaii and Puerto Rico of frozen fruits, effective September 15, 1937, have been issued by the Secretary of Agriculture under the authority of plant quarantines 13, 56, and 58.

Copies of these circulars have been sent to all collectors of customs for their information and guidance.

The number of this Treasury decision should be inserted as a marginal reference opposite articles 578 (b) (1), 579 and 580 (a) of the Customs Regulations of 1937.

JAMES H. MOYLE,
Commissioner of Customs.

ANNOUNCEMENTS RELATING TO JAPANESE BEETLE QUARANTINE (NO. 48)

B. P. Q. 359, Supplement No. 2.

INSTRUCTIONS TO INSPECTORS ON THE TREATMENT OF NURSERY PRODUCTS, FRUITS, VEGETABLES, AND SOIL, FOR THE JAPANESE BEETLE

OCTOBER 15, 1937.

Section II of Circular B. P. Q.–359 entitled, "Instructions to Inspectors on the Treatment of Nursery Products, Fruits, Vegetables, and Soil, for the Japanese Beetle," is further supplemented as follows:

II. TREATMENT OF SOIL ABOUT THE ROOTS OF PLANTS

F. PARADICHLOROBENZENE TREATMENT

The following instructions, based on the horizontal diffusion of gaseous paradichlorobenzene, do not supplant the instructions given in supplement No. 1 to B. P. Q.–359, issued August 23, 1935, but modify them in such a manner that the treatment can be applied more safely to the smaller sizes of nursery plants.

Material.—Paradichlorobenzene. A technical grade or C. P. grade, ground into small-sized crystals, is satisfactory for this treatment.

Condition of plunging soil.—Paradichlorobenzene should be mixed with a light soil, which should be moist, friable, and relatively low in organic matter. It should be sifted through a half-inch mesh screen to remove large lumps, stones, and debris prior to mixing with paradichlorobenzene.

Condition of plant ball.—The plant balls should be moist, *but not wet*, and not over 6 inches in diameter. If the soil is wet the treatment will not be satisfactory; if the soil is dry the plants may be injured during the treatment.

Season.—Treatment can be made at any time between October 1 and May 1, providing the proper temperature conditions can be obtained.

Temperature, dosage, and exposure requirements.—The various combinations of temperature, dosage and exposure which are effective in destroying the larvae in plant balls of different diameters are given in table 5. The temperatures given at the head of the different columns in table 5 are considered to be the minimum temperature during the treatment.

Application of the treatment.—The treating-soil should be mixed immediately before being used, as follows: Spread the soil in a thin layer on a smooth surface of a floor, bench, or other suitable space, scatter the crystals uniformly over the surface of the soil, and mix thoroughly by means of a shovel, rake, hoe, or fork, turning the mass at least three times during the operation. It is necessary to remove the pots from potted plants before placing them in the treated soil. When the burlap on balled plants is of a coarse weave which will not inhibit the proper penetration of the gas, it may be left on the balls, but when the material is closely woven it should be removed. When the plants are ready for treatment, a layer of the treated soil is spread on a smooth hard surface such as a floor or bench. Then, a row of plants is placed on this soil with the balls spaced at least 1 inch apart. Then the spaces between the plant balls are filled with treated soil, taking care not to get it on top of the balls or in contact with the stems. Finally, about 1 inch of treated soil is placed firmly against the row of treated plants. The operation is repeated until all of the plants are in place. When completed, each plant ball is surrounded on the sides and bottom by at least 1 inch of treated soil.

Care of plants during treatment.—The plants should not be removed from the treated soil during the period of the treatment. If it is necessary to apply water to the plants during the treatment to prevent desiccation, the operation should be limited to a light syringing, under the supervision of an inspector. If sufficient water is applied to make the treated soil or the plant balls muddy, the insecticidal action of the gas may be seriously impaired.

Care of plants after treatment.—The insecticidal action of the gas is completed at the end of the period of treatment. It is advisable to avoid excessive watering of the plants after removing them from the treated soil in order to permit any residual gas to escape from the plant balls. Saturating the balls with water tends to prevent the escape of this residual gas and may cause some injury to the plants. It is possible to handle the plants after treatment by the usual nursery procedure, providing care is taken to avoid reinfestation.

TABLE 5.—*Dosage, temperature, and exposure requirements for paradichlorobenzene to destroy larvae of the Japanese beetle by horizontal diffusion of the gas through plant balls of different widths*

Diameter of the plant balls (inches)	Crystals per cubic yard of plunging soil	Treatment required when the minimum temperature is within the range of—					
		45°–49° F.	50°–54° F.	55°–59° F.	60°–64° F.	65°–69° F.	70°–74° F.
	Pounds	*Days*	*Days*	*Days*	*Days*	*Days*	*Days*
Up to 2	1	(1)	----------	10	9	7	5
	5	9	7	6	5	4	2
	10	7	6	5	4	3	2
	20	5	5	4	3	2	1
2–4	1	----------	----------	----------	----------	10	6
	5	----------	10	10	9	8	4
	10	9	8	8	7	6	3
	20	7	7	6	6	5	2
4–6	1	----------	----------	----------	----------	----------	----------
	5	----------	----------	----------	----------	----------	----------
	10	----------	----------	----------	----------	9	7
	20	----------	----------	----------	8	7	4

¹ Leaders indicate that the exposure is more than 10 days.

Varieties of plants.—In addition to the varieties of azaleas—*Azalea hinodigiri, A. amoena, A. obtusa kiusiana* var. Coral Bells, *A. kaempferi* vars. Cleopatra, Fedora, Othello, and Salmon Beauty, for which the treatment was originally recommended, the preliminary experiments indicate that the following varieties of plants might be treated satisfactorily by this procedure: *Anemone hupehensis, Acquilegia* sp. var. Mrs. Scott Elliott's hybrid, *Artemisia dracunculus, Aster alpinis, Campanula medium, Ceratostigma plumbaginoides, Chrysanthemum* sp., *Dianthus caryophyllus* var. Abbotsford Pink, *Digitalis purpurea, Eupatorium coelestinum, Helianthemum glaucum croceum, Iberis amara, Myosotis* sp., *Pachysandra terminalis, Phlox* sp. var. R. P. Struthers, *Santolina chamaecyparissus incana, Sedum acre, Sempervivum alberti, Stokesia laevis, Thymus serpyllum, Viola* sp. var. Jersey Gem, and *Viola* sp. var. Rosina.

The treatment of the following varieties of potted plants by this procedure is still somewhat doubtful: *Cerastium biebersteini, Delphinium grandiflorum chinense, Fragaria* sp. vars. Bun Special, Dorse, Fairfax, and Joe, *Limonium latifolium, Papaver nudicaule, P. orientale,* and *Primula veris.*

LEE A. STRONG,
Chief, Bureau of Entomology and Plant Quarantine.

B. P. Q. 359, Supplement No. 3.

INSTRUCTIONS TO INSPECTORS ON THE TREATMENT OF NURSERY PRODUCTS, FRUITS, VEGETABLES, AND SOIL, FOR THE JAPANESE BEETLE

DECEMBER 20, 1937.

Section II of Circular B. P. Q. 359 entitled, "Instructions to Inspectors on the Treatment of Nursery Products, Fruits, Vegetables, and Soil, for the Japanese Beetle," is further supplemented as follows:

II. TREATMENT OF SOIL ABOUT THE ROOTS OF PLANTS

G. FUMIGATION OF STRAWBERRY PLANTS FOR JAPANESE BEETLE LARVAE

The treatment outlined herein may be employed as a basis for certification of strawberry plants under regulation 6 of Quarantine No. 48 (twelfth revision).

Fumigation with methyl bromide at a dosage of 3 pounds per 1,000 cubic feet, including the space occupied by the strawberry plants, for a period of 4 hours, the plants and room to be at a temperature of not less than 60° F. during the fumigation period. The treatment is to be applied in a tight room with gas-tight doors, and the strawberry plants shall be piled loosely in open crates or baskets and stacked in the room so that the gas mixture can have access to all sides of the container. After the room is loaded and closed the dosage of methyl bromide shall be volatilized within the room. The air-gas mixture shall be circulated by means of a fan or blower throughout the entire 4-hour fumigation period, and the treatment is to be applied in a fumigation chamber of approved design and under the supervision of an inspector of the Bureau of Entomology and Plant Quarantine of the United States Department of Agriculture.

In authorizing the movement of strawberry plants fumigated according to the requirements stated above, it is to be understood that no liability shall attach either to the United States Department of Agriculture or to any of its employees in the event of injury resulting to the strawberry plants.

Caution.—Methyl bromide is a gas at ordinary temperatures. It is colorless and practically odorless in concentrations used for fumigation of strawberry plants. It is a poison, and the operator should use an approved gas mask when exposed to the gas at concentrations used in fumigation. The strawberry plants in the fumigation chamber should be well aerated by blowing air through them and by ventilating the house before it is entered and the plants removed.

AVERY S. HOYT,
Acting Chief, Bureau of Entomology and Plant Quarantine.

ANNOUNCEMENTS RELATING TO MEXICAN FRUITFLY QUARANTINE (NO. 64)

MEXICAN FRUITFLY QUARANTINE

REVISION OF QUARANTINE AND REGULATIONS

INTRODUCTORY NOTE

The following revision of Federal Domestic Plant Quarantine No. 64 and regulations supplemental thereto adds a portion of Jim Wells County in Texas to the regulated area; fixes a host-free period from May 1 to August 31, inclusive, of each year, subject to such modifications as to duration and dates of commencement and termination as may be authorized by the Chief of the Bureau of Entomology and Plant Quarantine; designates the insect formerly known as Mexican fruitworm under the more appropriate title of Mexican fruitfly; adds fruits of species of the genus *Sargentia* to the list of hosts; modifies former specific restrictions as to containers; and provides that the Chief of the Bureau of Entomology and Plant Quarantine may specify the conditions and period for the maintenance of sanitary requirements in groves, and may modify, by administrative instructions, any of the restrictions contained in the regulations, other than those pertaining to extension or reduction of the regulated area, when in his judgment such action is necessary to prevent the spread of the Mexican fruitfly.

SUMMARY

These regulations as revised prohibit the interstate shipment of grapefruit, oranges, and all other citrus fruits except lemons and sour limes, from the counties of Brooks, Cameron, Hidalgo, Willacy, and a portion of Jim Wells County, Tex., unless a Federal permit (Form 443) has been issued therefor. The permits may be limited as to destination, and when so limited, are not valid for shipment to other destination points or areas (except to diversion points for diversion to authorized destinations only) (regulation 5 (*a*)).

Peaches, apples, pears, plums, quinces, apricots, mangoes, sapotas, guavas, mameys, ciruelas, and fruit of species of the genus *Sargentia* are prohibited interstate shipment from the regulated area (regulations 1 (*c*) and 5 (*b*)).

There are no restrictions on the shipment of lemons or sour limes (regulation 5 (*c*)).

Sterilization may be required as a condition for interstate movement of host fruits from defined infested zones (regulation 6 (e)).

A host-free period is to be maintained from May 1 to August 31, inclusive (regulation 7 (sec. A)).

Information relative to the issuance and use of permits is given in regulations 6 and 7.

LEE A. STRONG,
Chief, Bureau of Entomology and Plant Quarantine.

NOTICE OF QUARANTINE NO. 64 (REVISED)

[Approved October 15, 1937; effective October 15, 1937]

I, Henry A. Wallace, Secretary of Agriculture, have determined that it is necessary to quarantine the State of Texas to prevent the spread of an injurious insect known as the Mexican fruitfly (*Anastrepha ludens* Loew), new to and not heretofore widely prevalent or distributed within and throughout the United States.

Now, therefore, under authority conferred by the Plant Quarantine Act of August 20, 1912 (37 Stat. 315), as amended by the act of Congress approved March 4, 1917 (39 Stat. 1134, 1165), and having duly given the public hearing required thereby, I do quarantine the said State of Texas, effective on and after October 15, 1937, and by this Notice of Quarantine No. 64 do order that no fruits of any variety shall be shipped, offered for shipment to a common carrier, received for transportation, or carried by a common carrier, or carried, transported, moved, or allowed to be moved interstate from the said quarantined State in manner or method or under conditions other than those prescribed in the rules and regulations promulgated pursuant thereto or under such modification thereof as may be issued by the Chief of the Bureau of Entomology and Plant Quarantine as hereinafter provided: *Provided,* That the restrictions of this quarantine and of the rules and regulations supplemental thereto or modification thereof as hereinafter provided, may be limited to the areas in the State of Texas now, or which may hereafter be, designated by the Secretary of Agriculture as regulated areas: *Provided further,* That such limitation of the restrictions to the regulated areas shall be conditioned upon the said State providing for and enforcing such control measures with respect to such regulated areas, including the control of intrastate movement of host fruits from such areas, as in the judgment of the Secretary of Agriculture shall be deemed adequate to prevent the spread of the Mexican fruitfly therefrom to other parts of the State: *And provided further,* That, except as to extension or reduction of the regulated area, the Chief of the Bureau of Entomology and Plant Quarantine may modify by administrative instructions any of the restrictions of the regulations supplemental hereto when in his judgment such action is necessary to prevent the spread of the Mexican fruitfly.

Done at the city of Washington this 15th day of October 1937.

Witness my hand and the seal of the United States Department of Agriculture.

[SEAL]   H. A. WALLACE,
                                        Secretary of Agriculture.

RULES AND REGULATIONS (SECOND REVISION) SUPPLEMENTAL TO NOTICE OF QUARANTINE NO. 64

[Approved October 15, 1937; effective October 15, 1937]

REGULATION 1. DEFINITIONS

For the purpose of these regulations, the following words shall be construed respectively to mean:

(a) *Mexican fruitfly.*—The insect known as the Mexican fruitfly (*Anastrepha ludens* Loew).

(b) *Regulated areas.*—The areas in the State of Texas now, or which may hereafter be, designated as such by the Secretary of Agriculture in accordance with the provisos to Notice of Quarantine No. 64.

(c) *Host fruits.*—Fruits susceptible to infestation by the Mexican fruitfly, namely, mangoes, sapotas (including sapodillas and the fruit of all members of the family Sapotaceae and of the genus *Casimiroa* and all other fruits commonly called sapotas or sapotes), peaches, guavas, apples, pears, plums, quinces, apricots, mameys, ciruelas, fruit of species of the genus *Sargentia*, and all citrus fruits except lemons and sour limes, together with any other fruits which may later be determined as susceptible and of which due notice will be given.

(*d*) *Host-free period.*—A period of time during which no host fruits are produced or permitted to exist within the regulated area, except immature fruit in such stage of development, and mature fruit held or stored under such conditions as are prescribed by the Chief of the Bureau of Entomology and Plant Quarantine, which in his judgment do not convey risk of propagating the Mexican fruitfly.

(*e*) *Inspector.*—An inspector of the United States Department of Agriculture.

(*f*) *Moved interstate.*—Shipped, offered for shipment to a common carrier, received for transportation or transported by a common carrier, or carried, transported, moved, or allowed to be moved from the area designated as regulated in the State of Texas into or through any other State or Territory or District.

REGULATION 2. LIMITATION OF RESTRICTIONS TO REGULATED AREAS

Conditioned upon the compliance on the part of the State of Texas with the provisos to Notice of Quarantine No. 64, the restrictions provided in these regulations or subsequent administrative instructions on the production or interstate movement of fruit will be limited to fruit produced in or moving interstate from the areas in Texas now or hereafter designated by the Secretary of Agriculture as regulated areas.

REGULATION 3. REGULATED AREA

In accordance with the provisos to Notice of Quarantine No. 64, the Secretary of Agriculture designates as "regulated area" the counties of Brooks, Cameron, Hidalgo, and Willacy in the State of Texas, and that portion of Jim Wells County, Tex., lying south of Highway 141 and a line projected due west to the Jim Wells-Duval County line from the point where Highways 141 and 66 intersect, including all cities, towns, townships, and other political subdivisions within this area.

REGULATION 4. EXTENSION OR REDUCTION OF REGULATED AREAS

The regulated areas designated in regulation 3 may be extended or reduced as may be deemed advisable by the Secretary of Agriculture in accordance with the provisions of the Plant Quarantine Act of August 20, 1912, as amended.

REGULATION 5. RESTRICTIONS ON THE INTERSTATE MOVEMENT OF FRUIT FROM THE REGULATED AREA

(*a*) *Permits required.*—Grapefruit, oranges, and other citrus fruits (except as provided in paragraph (*c*) hereof) shall not be moved interstate from a regulated area into or through any point outside thereof unless a permit has been issued therefor by the United States Department of Agriculture.

(*b*) *Movement of noncitrus hosts prohibited.*—Peaches, apples, pears, plums, quinces, apricots, mangoes, sapotas (see regulation 1 (*c*)), guavas, mameys, ciruelas, and fruits of species of the genus *Sargentia* shall not be moved interstate from the regulated area and no permits will be issued for such movement.

(*c*) *No restrictions on immune and manufactured fruits.*—No restrictions are placed by these regulations on the interstate movement of lemons, sour limes, or other nonhost fruits, nor on the interstate movement of host fruits which have been manufactured or processed in such manner as to eliminate danger of carrying the Mexican fruitfly.

(*d*) *Movement through regulated area.*—No restrictions are placed by these regulations on the interstate movement of restricted articles from an area not under regulation through a regulated area when such movement is on a through bill of lading.

REGULATION 6. CONDITIONS GOVERNING THE ISSUANCE OF PERMITS

Permits for the interstate movement of grapefruit, oranges, and other restricted citrus fruits from the regulated area may be issued upon determination by the inspector that the proposed movement does not involve risk of spread of the Mexican fruitfly. Such determination will be based on compliance with the following conditions:

(a) *Grove inspection and sanitation.*—The grove in which the fruit was produced shall be maintained in compliance with the host-free requirement of these regulations and shall be kept free from drops and windfalls during such periods and time as the Chief of the Bureau of Entomology and Plant Quarantine may direct. Such drops and windfalls shall be buried under at least 18 inches of tamped soil or otherwise disposed of in manner and method prescribed by the Chief of the Bureau of Entomology and Plant Quarantine. The grove shall further be maintained in compliance with such other requirements as may be enforced by the State of Texas for the suppression of Mexican fruitfly infestation. Permits may be issued for the interstate movement of fruit produced only in such groves as have been inspected within 30 days prior to the movement of the fruit concerned and have been found free from Mexican fruitfly infestation.

(b) *Packing-house requirements.*—The packer and shipper shall maintain his packing plant in compliance with the sanitation requirements of the State of Texas issued for the suppression of the Mexican fruitfly. The packer shall also maintain a complete record of all receipts and sales or shipments of host fruits, subject to examination by the inspector.

(c) *Applications.*—Persons desiring to purchase, pack, or move grapefruit, oranges, or other restricted citrus fruits interstate from the regulated area shall make application for a permit to the office of the Bureau of Entomology and Plant Quarantine, Harlingen, Tex., as far as possible in advance of the probable date of shipment. Applications shall show the nature and quantity of the fruit it is proposed to move, together with the location at which it will be packed, the name and address of the shipper, and a list of all groves, together with the names and addresses of the owners, from which fruit for packing will be secured. Each applicant shall file with his application a signed statement in which he agrees to notify the inspector of all additional groves from which fruit for packing will be secured, not to pack or ship fruit from any grove until he has received written notification from the inspector that the grove has been maintained in compliance with the regulations issued under this quarantine, and to discontinue packing and shipping the fruit from any grove on notification from the inspector of the discovery of an infestation of the Mexican fruitfly in such grove or adjoining groves or of failure on the part of the owner or manager of such grove to comply with any condition of these regulations.

(d) *Containers.*—Permits will be issued for the interstate movement of only such fruit as is packed in containers customarily used in the regulated area for the commercial shipment of citrus fruits, and which are of such nature as will permit the inspector to identify the contents thereof.

(e) *Sterilization may be required.*—Sterilization of host fruits in manner and by method prescribed by the Chief of the Bureau of Entomology and Plant Quarantine may be required as a condition for the issuance of permits for interstate movement thereof when in his judgment the shipments concerned might involve risk of spread of the Mexican fruitfly.

(f) *Destination limitations.*—Permits may be limited as to destination and when so limited the fruits covered thereby shall not be moved interstate from the regulated area, directly or indirectly, either in the original containers or otherwise, to destinations other than those authorized in such permits, except to the usual diversion points for diversion to authorized destinations only.

(g) *Cancelation of permits.*—Any permits issued under these regulations may be withdrawn or canceled and further permits refused either for any failure of compliance with these regulations or violation of them, or whenever in the judgment of the inspector the further use of such permits might result in the dissemination of infestation.

REGULATION 7. CONDITIONS REQUIRED IN THE REGULATED AREAS

The interstate movement of grapefruit, oranges, and other restricted citrus fruit from the regulated areas under permits issued by the United States Department of Agriculture will be conditioned on the State of Texas providing for and enforcing the following control measures in manner and by method approved by, the United States Department of Agriculture, namely:

SECTION A. HOST-FREE PERIOD

A host-free period shall be maintained each year beginning on the first day of May and continuing until the first day of September, subject to such modification as to duration and dates of commencement and termination as may be authorized, by the Chief of the Bureau of Entomology and Plant Quarantine when in his judgment such modification does not involve increased risk of spread of the Mexican fruitfly.

Prior to the commencement of such host-free period each year, all restricted citrus fruit shall be removed from the tree for immediate sale or shipment, or for retention in flyproof storage approved by the Chief of the Bureau of Entomology and Plant Quarantine, and all other host fruits shall be destroyed either following removal from the trees or by destruction of the trees themselves.

No host fruits shall be permitted to remain on trees or to exist elsewhere within a regulated area at any time during such host-free period except immature citrus fruits which in the judgment of the Chief of the Bureau of Entomology and Plant Quarantine are not susceptible to infestation by the Mexican fruitfly.

SECTION B. INSPECTION

A system of inspection shall be carried on throughout the year to provide for the efficient enforcement of sections A and C of this regulation, for the prompt discovery of any infestations which occur, and for the enforcement of such conditions in and around citrus groves and packing and processing plants as shall be necessary to prevent the dissemination of Mexican fruitfly through the interstate movement of citrus host fruits.

SECTION C. INFESTED ZONES

Upon the determination of a Mexican fruitfly infestation within a regulated area, which in the judgment of the Chief of the Bureau of Entomology and Plant Quarantine constitutes a risk of spread of such fly, an infested zone shall be designated by the State of Texas subject to approval by the United States Department of Agriculture and all host fruits in susceptible stages of maturity produced within such zone and existing in the regulated area shall be destroyed or processed in such a manner as to render them free from infestation.

REGULATION 8. MARKING REQUIREMENTS

Every crate, box, or other container of host fruit moved interstate under these regulations shall have securely attached thereto a shipping permit (Form 443) issued under the provisions of regulation 6, and shall be subject to such other marking as may be required by the inspector.

Each shipment of six or more crates, boxes, or other containers of host fruit moved interstate under these regulations shall, in addition to the shipping permit on each such container, be accompanied by a master permit (Form 515) showing the number of containers and either the license number and destination of the vehicle or the name, number, and destination of the freight car or other carrier, as the case may be.

REGULATION 9. INSPECTION IN TRANSIT

Any car, vehicle, basket, box, crate, or other container, moved interstate, which contains or which the inspector has probable cause to believe contains articles the movement of which is prohibited or restricted by these regulations, shall be subject to inspection by inspectors at any time or place.

REGULATION 10. SHIPMENTS BY THE UNITED STATES DEPARTMENT OF AGRICULTURE

Articles subject to restriction in these regulations may be moved interstate by the United States Department of Agriculture for experimental or scientific purposes, on such conditions and under such safeguards as may be prescribed by the Chief of the Bureau of Entomology and Plant Quarantine. The container of articles so moved shall bear, securely attached to the outside thereof, an identifying tag from the Bureau of Entomology and Plant Quarantine showing compliance with such conditions.

These revised rules and regulations shall be effective on and after October 15, 1937, and shall supersede the rules and regulations promulgated August 12. 1932, as amended.

Done at the city of Washington this 15th day of October 1937.

Witness my hand and the seal of the United States Department of Agriculture.

[SEAL]   H. A. WALLACE,
                                        Secretary of Agriculture.

[The foregoing revision was sent to all common carriers doing business in or through the State of Texas.]

NOTICE TO GENERAL PUBLIC THROUGH NEWSPAPERS

UNITED STATES DEPARTMENT OF AGRICULTURE,
BUREAU OF ENTOMOLOGY AND PLANT QUARANTINE,
Washington, D. C., October 14, 1937.

Notice is hereby given that the Secretary of Agriculture, under authority conferred on him by the Plant Quarantine Act of August 20, 1912 (37 Stat. 315), as amended, has promulgated a revision of Notice of Quarantine No. 64, on account of the Mexican fruitfly, and of the revised rules and regulations supplemental thereto, effective on and after October 15, 1937. The revision adds a portion of Jim Wells County in Texas to the regulated area; designates May 1 to August 31 inclusive, as the host-free period, and makes certain other minor changes. Copies of the revised quarantine and regulations may be obtained from the Bureau of Entomology and Plant Quarantine, Washington, D. C.

                                        H. A. WALLACE,
                                        Secretary of Agriculture.

[The above notice was published in the Brownsville Herald, Brownsville. Tex., October 25, 1937.]

INSTRUCTIONS TO POSTMASTERS

POST OFFICE DEPARTMENT,
THIRD ASSISTANT POSTMASTER GENERAL,
Washington, October 21, 1937.

Postmaster:

MY DEAR SIR: Your attention is invited to the inclosed copy of the latest revision of the Mexican fruitfly quarantine and regulations (Quarantine Order No 64 of the United States Department of Agriculture), by which you will please be governed. See paragraph 1, section 595, Postal Laws and Regulations.

Very truly yours,

                                        ROY M. NORTH,
                                        Acting Third Assistant Postmaster General.

ANNOUNCEMENTS RELATING TO PINK BOLLWORM QUARANTINE (NO. 52)

MODIFICATION OF PINK BOLLWORM QUARANTINE REGULATIONS

INTRODUCTORY NOTE

The following revision adds the counties of Socorro and Valencia in New Mexico to the lightly infested areas. There are no ginning facilities in these counties and the small amount of cotton grown therein is carried into the adjacent regulated area for ginning. The inclusion of these counties in the regulated area allows such seed to be returned after ginning to farms and ranches in

Socorro and Valencia Counties for planting and feeding purposes.   No other
changes are made in the regulations.

LEE A. STRONG,
Chief, Bureau of Entomology and Plant Quarantine.

AMENDMENT NO. 3 TO REVISED RULES AND REGULATIONS SUPPLEMENTAL TO NOTICE OF QUARANTINE NO. 52

[Approved October 27, 1937; effective October 28, 1937]

Under authority conferred by the Plant Quarantine Act of August 20, 1912
(37 Stat. 315), as amended by the act of Congress approved March 4, 1917 (39
Stat. 1134, 1165), it is ordered that regulation 3 of the revised rules and regulations supplemental to Notice of Quarantine No. 52 on account of the pink bollworm of cotton, which were promulgated on October 13, 1936, as amended effective December 1, 1936, and further amended effective April 6, 1937, be and the
same is hereby still further amended to read as follows:

REGULATION 3. REGULATED AREAS; HEAVILY AND LIGHTLY INFESTED AREAS

REGULATED AREAS

In accordance with the provisos to Notice of Quarantine No. 52 (revised), the
Secretary of Agriculture designates as regulated areas, for the purpose of these
regulations, the following counties in Arizona, New Mexico, and Texas, including
all cities, districts, towns, townships, and other political subdivisions within
their limits:

Arizona area.—Counties of Cochise, Graham, and Greenlee.

New Mexico area.—Counties of Chaves, Dona Ana, Eddy, Grant, Hidalgo, Lea,
Luna, Otero, Roosevelt, Sierra, Socorro, and Valencia.

Texas area.—Counties of Andrews, Brewster, Cameron, Cochran, Crane, Culberson, Dawson, Ector, El Paso, Gaines, Glasscock, Hidalgo, Hockley, Howard,
Hudspeth, Jeff Davis, Loving, Martin, Midland, Pecos, Presidio, Reeves, Starr,
Terrell, Terry, Upton, Ward, Willacy, Winkler, and Yoakum; that part of *Bailey
County* lying south of the following-described boundary line: beginning on the
east line of said county where the county line intersects the northern boundary
line of league 207; thence west following the northern boundary line of leagues
207, 203, 191, 188, 175, and 171 to the northeast corner of league 171; thence
south on the western line of league 171 to the northeast corner of the W. H. L.
survey; thence west along the northern boundary of the W. H. L. survey and the
northern boundary of sections 68, 67, 66, 65, 64, 63, 62, 61, and 60 of block A of
the M. B. & B. survey to the western boundary of said county; that part of *Lamb
County* lying south of the following-described boundary line: beginning on the
east line of said county where the county line intersects the northern boundary
line of section 9 of the R. M. Thomson survey; thence west following the northern
boundary line of sections 9 and 10 of the R. M. Thomson survey and the northern
boundary line of sections 6, 5, 4, 3, 2, and 1 of the T. A. Thompson survey and the
northern boundary line of leagues 637, 636, and 635 to the southeast corner of
league 239; thence north on the eastern boundary line of league 239 to the northeast corner of said league; thence west on the northern boundary line of leagues
239, 238, 233, 222, 218, and 207 to the western boundary line of said county.

HEAVILY INFESTED AREAS

Of the regulated areas, the following counties and parts of counties are hereby designated as heavily infested within the meaning of these regulations:

Counties of Brewster, Culberson, Jeff Davis, Presidio, and Terrell, in the State
of Texas, and all of *Hudspeth County* in the same State except that part of the
northwest corner of said county lying north and west of a ridge of desert land
extending from the banks of the Rio Grande northeasterly through the desert
immediately west of the town of McNary, such ridge being an extension of the
northwest boundary line of section 11, block 65½.

LIGHTLY INFESTED AREAS

The following areas are designated as lightly infested:

The counties of Cochise, Graham, and Greenlee in Arizona;[1] the counties of Chaves, Dona Ana, Eddy, Grant, Hidalgo, Lea, Luna, Otero, Roosevelt, Sierra, Socorro, and Valencia in New Mexico; the entire counties of Andrews, Cameron, Cochran, Crane, Dawson, Ector, El Paso, Gaines, Glasscock, Hidalgo, Hockley, Howard, Loving, Martin, Midland, Pecos, Reeves, Starr, Terry, Upton, Ward, Willacy, Winkler, and Yoakum, the regulated parts of Bailey and Lamb Counties in Texas, and that part of the northwest corner of Hudspeth County, Tex., lying north and west of a ridge of desert land extending from the banks of the Rio Grande northeasterly through the desert immediately west of the town of McNary, such ridge being an extension of the northwest boundary line of section 11, block 65½.

This amendment shall be effective on and after October 28, 1937, and shall on that date supersede amendment No. 2 which became effective April 6, 1937.

Done at the city of Washington this 27th day of October 1937.

Witness my hand and the seal of the United States Department of Agriculture.

[SEAL]　　　　　　　　　　　　　　　　　　　　HARRY L. BROWN,
　　　　　　　　　　　　　　　　　　　Acting Secretary of Agriculture.

[The foregoing amendment was sent to all common carriers doing business in or through the States of Texas, New Mexico, and Arizona.]

NOTICE TO GENERAL PUBLIC THROUGH NEWSPAPERS

UNITED STATES DEPARTMENT OF AGRICULTURE,
BUREAU OF ENTOMOLOGY AND PLANT QUARANTINE,
Washington, D. C., October 28, 1937.

Notice is hereby given that the Secretary of Agriculture, under authority conferred on him by the Plant Quarantine Act of August 20, 1912 (37 Stat. 315), as amended, has promulgated amendment No. 3 to the revised rules and regulations supplemental to Notice of Quarantine No. 52, on account of the pink bollworm of cotton, effective on and after October 28, 1937. The purpose of the amendment is to add to the lightly infested areas the counties of Socorro and Valencia in New Mexico. Copies of the amendment may be obtained from the Bureau of Entomology and Plant Quarantine, United States Department of Agriculture, Washington, D. C.

　　　　　　　　　　　　　　　　　　　　HARRY L. BROWN,
　　　　　　　　　　　　　　　　　　　Acting Secretary of Agriculture.

[The above notice was published in the Journal, Albuquerque, N. Mex., November 8, 1937.]

INSTRUCTIONS TO POSTMASTERS

POST OFFICE DEPARTMENT,
THIRD ASSISTANT POSTMASTER GENERAL,
Washington, November 5, 1937.

Postmaster:

MY DEAR SIR: Your attention is invited to the inclosed copy of Plant Quarantine No. 52 of the United States Department of Agriculture, on account of the pink bollworm of cotton, and also a copy of revised regulation 3 in connection therewith, effective October 28, 1937, by which you will please be governed. See paragraph 1, section 595, Postal Laws and Regulations.

The revision extends the regulated area, adding the counties of Socorro and Valencia in New Mexico to the area designated as lightly infested by the pink bollworm.

Very truly yours,

　　　　　　　　　　　　　　　　　　　　ROY M. NORTH,
　　　　　　　　　　　　　　　　　Acting Third Assistant Postmaster General.

---

[1] Part of the lightly infested area in Arizona is regulated on account of the Thurberia weevil under quarantine No. 61, and shipments therefrom must comply with the requirements of that quarantine.

MODIFICATION OF PINK BOLLWORM QUARANTINE REGULATIONS

INTRODUCTORY NOTE

The following revision adds Santa Cruz County in Arizona and portions of Pima and Pinal Counties in the same State hereinafter described to the lightly infested areas, on account of the recent discovery of the light pink bollworm infestation. No other changes are made in the regulations.

LEE A. STRONG,
Chief, Bureau of Entomology and Plant Quarantine.

AMENDMENT NO. 4 TO REVISED RULES AND REGULATIONS SUPPLEMENTAL TO NOTICE OF QUARANTINE NO. 52.

[Approved December 29, 1937; effective January 3, 1938]

Under authority conferred by the Plant Quarantine Act of August 20, 1912 (37 Stat. 315), as amended by the act of Congress approved March 4, 1917 (39 Stat. 1134, 1165), it is ordered that regulation 3 of the revised rules and regulations supplemental to Notice of Quarantine No. 52, on account of the pink bollworm of cotton, which were promulgated on October 13, 1936, as amended effective December 1, 1936, further amended effective April 6, 1937, and further amended effective October 28, 1937, be and the same is hereby still further amended to read as follows:

REGULATION 3. REGULATED AREAS; HEAVILY AND LIGHTLY INFESTED AREAS

REGULATED AREAS

In accordance with the provisos to Notice of Quarantine No. 52 (revised), the Secretary of Agriculture designates as regulated areas, for the purpose of these regulations, the following counties in Arizona, New Mexico, and Texas, including all cities, districts, towns, townships, and other political subdivisions within their limits:

Arizona area.—Counties of Cochise, Graham, Greenlee, and Santa Cruz, all of *Pima County* except that part lying west of the western boundary line of range 8 east, and all of *Pinal County* except that part lying north of the northern boundary line of township 5 south, and west of State highways 87 and 187.

New Mexico area.—Counties of Chaves, Dona Ana, Eddy, Grant, Hidalgo, Lea, Luna, Otero, Roosevelt, Sierra, Socorro, and Valencia.

Texas area.—Counties of Andrews, Brewster, Cameron, Cochran, Crane, Culberson, Dawson, Ector, El Paso, Gaines. Glasscock, Hidalgo, Hockley, Howard, Hudspeth, Jeff Davis, Loving, Martin, Midland, Pecos, Presidio, Reeves, Starr, Terrell, Terry, Upton, Ward, Willacy, Winkler, and Yoakum; that part of *Bailey County* lying south of the following-described boundary line: beginning on the east line of said county where the county line intersects the northern boundary line of league 207; thence west following the northern boundary line of leagues 207, 203, 191, 188, 175, and 171 to the northeast corner of league 171; thence south on the western line of league 171 to the northeast corner of the W. H. L. survey; thence west along the northern boundary of the W. H. L. survey and the northern boundary of sections 68, 67, 66, 65, 64, 63, 62, 61, and 60 of block A of the M. B. & B. survey to the western boundary of said county; that part of *Lamb County* lying south of the following-described boundary line: beginning on the east line of said county where the county line intersects the northern boundary line of section 9 of the R. M. Thomson survey; thence west following the northern boundary line of sections 9 and 10 of the R. M. Thomson survey and the northern boundary line of sections 6, 5, 4, 3, 2, and 1 of the T. A. Thompson survey and the northern boundary line of leagues 637, 636, and 635 to the southeast corner of league 239; thence north on the eastern boundary line of league 239 to the northeast corner of said league; thence west on the northern boundary line of leagues 239, 238, 233, 222, 218, and 207 to the western boundary line of said county.

HEAVILY INFESTED AREAS

Of the regulated areas, the following counties and parts of counties are hereby designated as heavily infested within the meaning of these regulations:

Counties of Brewster, Culberson, Jeff Davis, Presidio, and Terrell, in the State of Texas, and all of *Hudspeth County* in the same State except that part of the northwest corner of said county lying north and west of a ridge of desert land extending from the banks of the Rio Grande northeasterly through the desert immediately west of the town of McNary, such ridge being an extension of the northwest boundary line of section 11, block 65½.

LIGHTLY INFESTED AREAS

The following areas are designated as lightly infested:

The counties of Cochise, Graham, Greenlee, and Santa Cruz, and the regulated parts of Pima and Pinal Counties in Arizona;[2] the counties of Chaves, Dona Ana, Eddy, Grant, Hidalgo, Lea, Luna, Otero, Roosevelt, Sierra, Socorro, and Valencia in New Mexico; the entire counties of Andrews, Cameron, Cochran, Crane, Dawson, Ector, El Paso, Gaines, Glasscock, Hidalgo, Hockley, Howard, Loving, Martin, Midland, Pecos, Reeves, Starr, Terry, Upton, Ward, Willacy, Winkler, and Yoakum, the regulated parts of Bailey and Lamb Counties in Texas, and that part of the northwest corner of Hudspeth County, Tex., lying north and west of a ridge of desert land extending from the banks of the Rio Grande northeasterly through the desert immediately west of the town of McNary, such ridge being an extension of the northwest boundary line of section 11, block 65½.

This amendment shall be effective on and after January 3, 1938, and shall on that date supersede amendment No. 3 which became effective October 28, 1937.

Done at the city of Washington this 29th day of December 1937.

Witness my hand and the seal of the United States Department of Agriculture.

[SEAL]

H. A. WALLACE,
Secretary of Agriculture.

[The foregoing amendment was sent to all common carriers doing business in or through the States of Texas, New Mexico, and Arizona.]

INSTRUCTIONS TO GENERAL PUBLIC THROUGH NEWSPAPERS

UNITED STATES DEPARTMENT OF AGRICULTURE,
BUREAU OF ENTOMOLOGY AND PLANT QUARANTINE,
Washington, D. C., December 29, 1937.

Notice is hereby given that the Secretary of Agriculture, under authority conferred on him by the Plant Quarantine Act of August 20, 1912 (37 Stat. 315), as amended, has promulgated amendment No. 4 to the revised rules and regulations supplemental to Notice of Quarantine No. 52 on account of the pink bollworm of cotton, effective on and after January 3, 1938. The purpose of the amendment is to add to the lightly infested area Santa Cruz County in Arizona and portions of Pima and Pinal Counties in the same State, not heretofore included. Copies of the amendment may be obtained from the Bureau of Entomology and Plant Quarantine, United States Department of Agriculture, Washington, D. C.

H. A. WALLACE,
Secretary of Agriculture.

[The above notice was published in the Republican, Phoenix, Ariz., January 10, 1938.]

ANNOUNCEMENT RELATING TO THURBERIA WEEVIL QUARANTINE (NO. 61)

B. E. P. Q.–436 (Revised).

ADMINISTRATIVE INSTRUCTIONS — APPROVAL OF ALTERNATIVE TREATMENTS FOR COTTONSEED AS A CONDITION FOR INTERSTATE MOVEMENT FROM THE AREA REGULATED UNDER QUARANTINE NO. 61

[Issued under regulation 6, Quarantine No. 61]

JULY 27, 1937.

Pursuant to authority vested in the Bureau of Entomology and Plant Quarantine under regulation 6 of the revised rules and regulations supplemental to

---

[2] Part of the lightly infested area in Arizona is regulated on account of the Thurberia weevil under quarantine No. 61, and shipments therefrom must comply with the requirements of that quarantine.

Notice of Quarantine No. 61, revised, which provides that permits may be issued for the interstate movement of cottonseed from the regulated area on such conditions as may be prescribed by that Bureau, the Bureau hereby approves any one of the following alternative treatments and permits may be issued for the interstate movement of cottonseed so treated:

When the cottonseed has been sterilized to 145° F. as a part of the continuous process of ginning and, in addition, has been treated by sulphuric acid and screening; or has been given a special heat treatment at 145° maintained under approved conditions for a period of thirty (30) minutes; or has been heated to a temperature of 155° in an approved manner separate and apart from ginning operations, and subsequent to any one of these treatments has been protected from contamination to the satisfaction of the inspector.

LEE A. STRONG,
Chief, Bureau of Entomology and Plant Quarantine.

ANNOUNCEMENT RELATING TO RULES AND REGULATIONS GOVERNING THE IMPORTATION OF COTTON AND COTTON WRAPPINGS INTO THE UNITED STATES

MODIFICATION OF COTTON REGULATIONS

AMENDMENT NO. 3 OF RULES AND REGULATIONS GOVERNING THE IMPORTATION OF COTTON AND COTTON WRAPPINGS INTO THE UNITED STATES

[Effective on and after December 11, 1937]

Under authority conferred by the Plant Quarantine Act of August 20, 1912 (37 Stat. 315), as amended, it is ordered that regulation 2 of the Rules and Regulations Governing the Importation of Cotton and Cotton Wrappings into the United States, as revised February 24, 1923, be, and the same is hereby, amended to read as follows:

REGULATION 2. APPLICATIONS FOR PERMITS

Persons contemplating the importation of cotton into the United States shall make application for a permit to the Secretary of Agriculture, Washington, D. C., in advance of shipment, on forms provided for that purpose.

Permits will authorize the entry of cotton at the ports of Boston, Providence, New York, Seattle, Portland, Oreg., San Francisco, and Los Angeles, and at such other ports of entry as may be approved by the Bureau of Entomology and Plant Quarantine:[3] *Provided,* That for cotton of the types not requiring disinfection as a condition of entry under the *proviso to regulation 6,* as modified effective May 1, 1924, and under the two *provisos to regulation 9,* and for second-hand burlap and other fabric of the kinds ordinarily used for wrapping cotton for which disinfection or approved equivalent treatment is not required under the *second proviso to regulation 11,* permits will be issued for entry at the following additional ports: Philadelphia, Baltimore, Norfolk, Charleston, Savannah, Mobile, Gulfport, Miss., New Orleans, Houston, Galveston, Beaumont, Port Arthur, Niagara Falls, Buffalo, Port Huron, Detroit, Chicago, and Sumas, Blaine, and Bellingham, Wash.: *Provided further,* That for second-hand burlap or other fabric of the kinds ordinarily used for wrapping cotton which is to be treated under conditions prescribed by the Bureau of Entomology and Plant Quarantine in a manner equivalent to disinfection under the *first proviso to regulation 11,* permits will be issued for entry at the additional ports of Philadelphia, Baltimore, Niagara Falls, Buffalo, Port Huron, Detroit, and Chicago.

Permits to authorize the entry of cotton via the United States for shipment to a foreign country will be issued under the provisions of the plant safeguard regulations for immediate exportation or for immediate transportation and exportation in bond as prescribed in the permit: *Provided,* That cotton which has been entered in bond for subsequent disinfection may be exported from the

---

[3] The Bureau of Entomology and Plant Quarantine has assumed the functions of the Federal Horticultural Board.

United States upon prior approval of, and under conditions to be prescribed by, the Bureau of Entomology, and Plant Quarantine.

(*a*) If cotton falling under these regulations is offered for entry at a port where the entry requirements cannot be met, provision must be made either for its prompt transfer to a port where the requirements of entry can be met, or for its removal forthwith from the port and the territorial waters of the United States. Transfers to other ports for compliance with the regulations, and the routing thereto, must be authorized by the Bureau of Entomology and Plant Quarantine.

(*b*) Under postal restrictions, the importation is authorized by samples, small packets, and parcel post of samples of raw or unmanufactured ginned cotton, including all forms of cotton-mill waste, when the parcels are securely wrapped to prevent leakage, and are conspicuously addressed to the United States Department of Agriculture, Bureau of Entomology and Plant Quarantine, at Washington, D. C., San Francisco, Calif., or Seattle, Wash., and, if from Mexico, at Nogales, Ariz., El Paso, Laredo, or Brownsville, Tex., with the name and address of the ultimate addressee indicated in the lower left-hand corner of the wrapper of the parcel. Upon receipt of the parcels at the designated inspection offices of the Bureau of Entomology and Plant Quarantine, they will be examined and disinfected, and forwarded to the ultimate addressee.

This amendment shall be effective on and after December 11, 1937.

Done at the city of Washington this 11th day of December 1937.

Witness my hand and the seal of the United States Department of Agriculture.

[SEAL]

H. A. WALLACE,
Secretary of Agriculture.

TERMINAL INSPECTION OF PLANTS AND PLANT PRODUCTS

ADDITIONAL PLANT INSPECTION PLACE IN CALIFORNIA

POST OFFICE DEPARTMENT,
THIRD ASSISTANT POSTMASTER GENERAL,
Washington, October 13, 1937.

Postmasters in the State of California are informed that provision has been made for the terminal inspection of plants and plant products at Nevada City, Nevada County, Calif., and this place should, therefore, be added to the list of places within the State of California to which plants and plant products subject to terminal inspection may be sent by postmasters for inspection under the provisions of section 596, Postal Laws and Regulations.

ROY M. NORTH,
Acting Third Assistant Postmaster General.

MISCELLANEOUS ITEMS

NURSERYMEN AND QUARANTINES

By LEE A. STRONG, *Chief, Bureau of Entomology and Plant Quarantine, United States Department of Agriculture*

[Given at the sixty-second annual meeting of the American Association of Nurserymen, Chicago, Ill., July 15, 1937]

The opportunity given to me by your president to talk to the American Association of Nurserymen is greatly appreciated. The nurserymen of America are as intimately associated with the affairs of the Bureau of Entomology and Plant Quarantine and as vitally concerned with its activities, accomplishments, and mistakes as is any group of agriculturists in the country.

During the past few years while the giving of work to unemployed and needy has been of the utmost importance, the Bureau of Entomology and Plant Quarantine has wherever possible made use of emergency funds to further the work of pest eradication and control. Since 1933, when the first emergency funds became available, until July 1, 1937, we have used $37,526,392 for such work

44332—38——3

and we have employed as many as 27,725 men at the peak, the average being 16,000. For the first 6 months of the current fiscal year an additional $4,660,564 of emergency relief funds has been provided. We have been able to step ahead by years the control and eradication of barberry, white-pine blister rust, citrus canker, phony peach, Dutch elm disease, pink bollworm, gypsy moth, and other features of control and eradication work.

One of the really important jobs under way at this time is the eradication of the Dutch elm disease which was first found in this country in 1930. Since that time in the inspection from the ground and by autogiro of millions of elm trees in the United States, there have been found to June 26, 1937, 22,898 trees in which the disease was confirmed. Of this number only 86 were found outside the main infected area in the vicinity of New York; namely, 33 at Cleveland, Ohio, 33 at Indianapolis, Ind., 1 at Cincinnati, Ohio, 1 at Cumberland, Md., 3 at Brunswick, Md., 2 at Baltimore, Md., 4 at Norfolk, Va., 1 at Portsmouth, Va., 1 at Guilford, Conn., 1 at Branford, Conn., and 6 at Old Lyme, Conn. In eliminating dead or dying trees in order to prevent building up of infestation by the beetle which carries the disease, 3,323,339 elm trees in a dead or dying condition from one cause or another have been removed. In this work up to June 30, 1937, $8,336,875 of emergency money and $672,312 regular money has been expended. For the first 6 months of the present fiscal year, an additional $1,724,040 of emergency relief funds has been provided, and $460,860 of regular funds has been appropriated for the current fiscal year. If permitted to continue in this work on the scale which its importance justifies, it is believed there is every reason to look forward to complete extermination of the disease in this country. Definite progress has been made and all the information we are able to obtain in this country and abroad indicates that the program we are pursuing is the only one which promises to be successful, and it does promise to be successful.

Of importance to the nurserymen everywhere is the Japanese beetle situation, and during the past season building up of infestation outside the quarantine area was not sufficiently important to warrant the extension in any marked degree of the quarantine area. Inevitably, unless something comes into the picture which we are not aware of, the Japanese beetle will ultimately spread to all those parts of the United States where it would find suitable environment. The job of enforcing the quarantine on account of the Japanese beetle is becoming more and more difficult and more and more complicated with an increasing number of people and industries affected. It is believed there is still justification for maintaining a Federal quarantine but sooner or later it would seem that the point would be reached where, by reason of large area or number of separate infestations, the Federal quarantine would no longer be warranted. This and other conditions having a bearing on the interstate movement of plant products bring forcibly to our attention the need and importance of bringing about a standardization and uniformity in inspection methods and quarantine activities of the States and of the Federal Government. That plant quarantines are necessary as a protection to uninfested and uninfected areas against major plant pests which are not established therein is generally recognized. The fact that quarantine action has been taken presupposes that a dangerous plant disease or insect pest is involved, the spread of which should be prevented; however the effectiveness of such quarantines depends on both enforcement and compliance. Enforcement rests with the officials while compliance is a function of the person moving the plants. In the enforcement of Federal quarantines we have assisted by supplementing the inspection forces in the control areas with transit inspection maintained at the more important transfer terminals for the purpose of intercepting shipments moving by freight, express, and mail in violation of quarantines. States also have at their disposal means for enforcing State quarantines although they are usually somewhat limited. In a number of States enforcement of quarantines is entirely inadequate due to lack of man power and other facilities. The effectiveness of quarantines in preventing the spread of dangerous plant pests under such conditions must depend pretty largely, if not entirely, on the compliance of the shippers and common carriers. As a whole, such people appreciate the value of pest control and are anxious to comply with quarantines but in many instances are not able to fully comply because of the numerous State quarantines now in existence which are complicated and involved as to procedure and subject matter covered in such quarantines. Do you know that there are now in existence over 200 separate and distinct State plant quarantines covering 52 plant pests? These include 32 State quarantines covering the subject of corn borer alone, no two of which are alike.

The alfalfa weevil is the subject of 25 State quarantines, all varying either as to infested area, commodities covered, or as to treatment of such commodities as a prerequisite of shipment. Similar conditions apply all the way down the line in practically every instance where more than one State has a quarantine against the same pest. There would seem to be no logical reason why 52 plant pests, now the subject of more than 200 State quarantines, could not be covered by 52 uniform quarantines, or why the 32 quarantines, now applying to the corn borer, could not be reduced to 1 quarantine, or the 25 now enforced against the alfalfa weevil could not be reduced to 1. If this cannot be done or if it is not done, what is going to be the situation with respect to the Japanese beetle quarantine if and when the Federal quarantine is given up? Standardization of inspection work and State quarantines can be accomplished and I am pleased to be able to say that the State quarantine officers, through their regional plant boards and through the National Plant Board in cooperation with the Bureau of Entomolgy and Plant Quarantine, or perhaps I should say assisted by the Bureau, are making progress in that direction. More progress is needed and I am sure it will come. The Bureau is now undertaking a careful review of each and every Federal quarantine in an attempt to simplify and clarify the wording and make more effective and more simple the working of each quarantine.

You have been familiar for several years with the work that has been done on the phony disease of peaches in the South. A newly discovered disease—peach mosaic—found for the first time at Brownwood, Tex., during 1931, has since been found in the States of Colorado, Utah, Arizona, New Mexico, Oklahoma, and California. It seems to be an extremely serious virus disease which may be artificially transmitted by budwood or peach bark grafts from either twig or root bark; hence, the most probable means of long-distance spread is through the medium of infected host plants or budding wood. The natural spread seems to be rapid and apparently occurs in colony formation. Eradication of this disease is looked upon as practicable if we may depend on evidence gained as a result of the work in Colorado and Utah, the only States where the eradication work has been energetically carried on a sufficient length of time to make accurate observations possible. The program on this disease and on the phony peach disease is carried on in cooperation with the States concerned and since August 1935, to date, 185,000 orchard trees, more than 6,500,000 abandoned orchard trees, and more than 55,000,000 escaped peach trees have been destroyed. Much more of this type of work could well be done in the interest of pest control in this country.

At the convention of this association in Chicago on July 20, 1933, I delivered an address to which I gave the rather imposing title of "The Past, Present, and Future of Quarantine 37." I pointed out what I thought were the bad features of the procedure we were following in enforcing the provisions of Quarantine 37, and while I did not indulge to any marked degree in crystal gazing in discussing the future of Quarantine 37, my limited entry into this field met with about the same success that most such efforts meet with. Following the delivery of this address a public conference was called in Washington on October 25, 1933, to reexamine the underlying principles involved in the interpretation and enforcement of Quarantine 37. It was specifically proposed to consider the elimination of consideration of the availability of plants in this country; limitation to be placed on the number of plants which may be imported by reason of facilities, or lack of the same, for adequate inspection; value of considering horticultural qualifications of applicants in the issuance of permits; desirability of continuing to hold certain plants for 2 or more years before release; the advisability of providing for the inspection of imported plants at New York and certain other ports of entry rather than shipping them to Washington as at present, and such other pertinent items as might be brought up. At this conference, as is usual with such conferences and public hearings, the sentiment of those in attendance was pretty largely moulded in advance of the conference by what might be termed paid representatives of special groups, and the fundamental principles of the quarantine were either discussed very superficially or not touched on at all. Aside from the comparatively few people who are interested commercially in the effects of the quarantine, those large masses of people who are affected in a small way individually but in a large way collectively, are seldom if ever represented at these conferences and public hearings and their real opinion is not therefore brought into public view. That was true of the conference held in October 1933.

It has been frequently noted that, in the words of the Federal Horticultural Board, Quarantine 37 voiced the policy of practical exclusion of plants if pests were to be excluded and thus necessarily of a given plant when that plant was known to be available in the United States. For the first few years following the promulgation of Quarantine 37, no attempt was made to establish definite quantity limits of imports. The volume of imports was controlled to some extent by selecting permittees and by refusing permits for what were believed to be available varieties. The public became more acquainted with the procedure for importing as time passed and consequently as the work grew, the need for quantity limits became apparent if the quarantine were to accomplish its announced purpose. Some rather liberal quantity limits were established during the fiscal year 1925 and these were somewhat reduced for the fiscal year 1926. No limits were placed on narcissus bulbs until the second year of importation under special permit. All the early limits applied to the varieties or in some cases, species, and importations were made cumulative in the fiscal year 1927, except for narcissus. Thus when an importer had entered the limit of a variety he would be refused permits for further importations of that variety. Narcissus limits were made cumulative in the fiscal year 1929. In the fiscal year 1930 the narcissus quantity limit was placed on a generic basis and the previous cumulative principle was abandoned for that genus. The same step was taken beginning with the fiscal year 1931 for all other genera. Between the fiscal years 1925 and 1931 there was a gradual lowering of quantity limits.

In establishing the quantity limits on a generic basis, the old bases, which differed for the amateur and commercial grower and as to the origin of material, were discarded and one set of limits was made to apply to all without regard to the origin of the material. While as noted although there had been a general and gradual reduction in limits from those first established in 1925 to the ones which became effective on July 1, 1930, it may be said that to a great extent the importers themselves set the new limits of July 1930. As a basis for formulating these new limits, analyses were made of the importations of genera principally imported and it was found that, broadly speaking, 100 plants of a genus of tree or shrub, 100 to 500 plants of a genus of herbaceous perennials, and 1,000 to 50,000 of a genus of bulbous and other root-crop genera would amply meet the needs of the importers as shown by actual records of their importations when limits were more liberal. Therefore, while the new limits appeared to involve drastic reductions, actually they fitted nicely with the importing habits of the public at that time. Habits of course formed as a result of the procedure followed in picking and choosing the few who should be given the privilege of monopoly in production of those varieties of plants embargoed and discouraging the thousands of individuals who would have liked and who merited the same privilege. Some consideration was given to the ease with which a kind of plant could be reproduced, its susceptibility to unfavorable transit conditions, the popular demand for it, but in view of the general restrictions effected by these limits, the question of pest risk—the real fundamental factor in question—was not considered in setting the limit on any one genus. Protests as to certain limitations were received and the limits were reviewed and in some instances revised with liberalizations, effective July 17, 1931.

When the limit of 100 plants was established for chrysanthemums and a limit of 250 was set for carnations, it did not mean that chrysanthemums involved any greater pest risk than carnations. The decision was made more on the basis of the relative ease of propagating the chrysanthemum. The placing of a limit of 500 for azaleas and rhododendrons, with a comparable limit of 100 for conifers, was based more on relative demand. Likewise, demand and purported horticultural difficulties influenced the placing of 50,000 for the limit of iris bulbs, while a limit of only 1,000 was established for oxalis.

When the limit was raised on July 17, 1931, from 1,000 to 5,000 for gladiolus and tuberous begonias and was not raised for gloxinias, the question of demand, not pest risk, entered into the picture. The fact that the limit on gloxinia was not likewise raised was due only and entirely to the lack of evidence that a need for greater liberality existed in the gloxinia limit. Some limits, as for example the one on delphinium, were raised largely because of the heavy losses from storage rots, heating, and other unfavorable transit conditions.

So much for the history of quantity limits. Their original purpose was in line with the announced purpose of Quarantine 37 namely, the ultimate exclusion of all stock not absolutely essential to the horticultural needs of the country. More recently they have been looked upon as justified only as a means for reducing the total volume of imports to that which could be adequately inspected by the personnel, and with the facilities available. They no longer serve even this purpose.

Early in the administration of the quarantine it was apparent that one importer might have good reason for wishing to place his importations in the care of another, where better propagating facilities, more favorable climatic conditions, etc., were available. A contract form signed by the importer and his agent and filed with the Department gained the sanction of the Department for such an arrangement. Doubtless there may have been an occasional effort to use this contractual arrangement as means of defeating the quantity limitations but certainly the practice was not general. Today the practice would seem to be in general use whenever the limits prevent one from importing the desired number of plants. It is known that certain firms have subsidiaries and, when the question of quantity limits is raised with the parent firm, the subsidiaries apply for and receive permits. Members of an importer's family, his employees, possibly his neighbors and friends, now apply in their own names, submitting contract forms with their applications. As an extreme illustration, which after all is extreme only in degree, I mention a firm which, in addition to importing the limit of a bulbous genus, contracted to grow, or allowed to be grown on its premises, the like importations of 27 other permittees. It is open to suspicion that one importer thus actually imported 28 times the quantity limit. Many other illustrations involving only fewer importations but accomplishing the same purpose of beating the quarantine, can be found in an examination of our files. Amateurs as well as commercial interests are involved because under our American system of Government one person is entitled as much as another to equal rights and privileges. It is obviously not within our province to attempt to say who shall import, as long as the importer agrees to utilize his imports for one of the purposes authorized under the quarantine. However, it is within our province to say and we do say here and now that, amateurs and individuals are entitled to and will receive the same consideration in the granting of permits as firms and corporations.

Since last appearing before you studies have been made of our means of determining the new varieties and necessary propagating stock, and the results achieved. According to our annual reports, at the close of the fiscal year 1922, 11,344 varieties of plants had been listed on special permit application forms—89.1 percent of these were approved for entry. By the close of the fiscal year 1933, 96.2 percent of the 62,570 varieties for which permits had been requested were approved for importation. In other words, while the net number of approved varieties had increased in those 11 years to nearly six times their number as of June 30, 1922, the net number of rejected varieties was less than two times the 1922 figure. On the other hand, hundreds of these approved varieties had not been listed on permit applications for many years. The trade had, in effect, "rejected" them as changing conditions, different architectural designs, new dress styles requiring flowers of various colors and types, and other shifting demands had brought about the need for the different, the newer, and often the better varieties. A review of the existing rejections, the majority of which had not been questioned by reason of later requests to import the varieties involved, showed that many so-called "rejected" varieties should be approved for entry. No new rejections were made and gradually we discontinued entirely, except for narcissus, the effort to designate varieties approved for entry. Insofar as varieties listed on applications for permit are concerned, the applications are now and will continue to be approved or disapproved solely on the basis of pest risk, in accord with the intent of the Plant Quarantine Act. This policy has been in effect for some time.

In selecting those applicants who should be approved to receive permits to import it was formerly necessary, in order to determine an applicant's horticultural qualifications, for him to show that he was an experienced grower of the type of plant desired and had ample facilities for the propagation of the proposed imports. Under this system there was little opportunity for the amateur to import, most importations being made by the larger commercial growers. Amateurs were approved on the basis of specializing in a genus, opening their estates to the public, and exhibiting at the larger horticultural shows. Hybridizers were handled on the same basis as amateurs, except that they were permitted, in the early days, to sell increase in the same manner as the commercial propagators. Beginning in 1926 there was a tendency toward greater liberality in establishing status, which culminated in the decision reached in this Bureau in 1934 to discontinue this phase of our procedure. It is questionable whether this Department had a right under the Plant Quarantine Act to say who is and who is not eligible to receive permits.

The wording of the regulations supplemental to Quarantine No. 37 explicitly states that certain importations are to be made for certain purposes which are in line with the original objective of the quarantine. I question whether they are in line with the wording of the act under which the quarantine was written. Nevertheless, the question of ultimate utilization of imports under special permit has always been intertwined with the procedure for administering that quarantine. With the discontinuance of the question of the applicant's horticultural qualifications to import, certain relaxations in the attitude toward utilization were obviously necessary. The quarantine makes no provision for entry under regulation 14 for immediate resale but almost any other proposed utilization could be, and is, construed as falling under the heading of one of the approved purposes. Consequently, insofar as utilization is concerned, no applications for special permits are denied except when it is known that immediate resale is contemplated. This liberalization brings the administration of the quarantine more nearly perhaps but not entirely into legal relation with the act.

The Plant Quarantine Act does not provide for any procedure whereby an importation once released at the port of entry must be grown under approved horticultural conditions for any period to give the Department opportunity for further inspections to determine apparent freedom from pests. Consequently, field inspections of special permit importations have been discontinued. I am not prepared to say, however, that in all cases there should be no follow-up field inspections but I repeat what I said in 1933—that inspection methods have improved, knowledge of conditions has been added to, and more reliance can now be placed in inspection at the time of entry than was the case in 1919 when the quarantine was promulgated. Importers are still required to sign the agreement to hold their imports for a period of at least 2 years.

I have attempted to detail the principal features that have been found to be out of harmony with the legal provisions of the Plant Quarantine Act, with present needs of the country and with sound quarantine practice. Most of these features ignore or disregard entirely the pest risk which should be the real basis of the quarantine.

Let us now turn for the moment to the quarantine itself to see what is necessary to bring it in harmony with the act.

In brief, section 1 of the Plant Quarantine Act requires that nursery stock imported or offered for entry must be imported under permit issued under such conditions as the Secretary of Agriculture may prescribe, in addition to those laid down in the act. Each shipment must be accompanied by a certificate of the proper official of the country from which the importation is made to the effect that it has been inspected and is believed to be free of pests. When the conditions prescribed by the Secretary of Agriculture have been met, it is mandatory for him to issue a permit for the importation. It is provided that the Secretary may prescribe regulations to govern the entry of nursery stock from countries not maintaining official systems of inspection. Importations by the Department of Agriculture may be made for experimental or scientific purposes under such regulations as may be prescribed by the Secretary of Agriculture. Please note that this section only provides for the Secretary to make conditions of entry. He may require that importations shall be free of pests and it is within his province to cause inspection to be made to determine compliance with this requirement. He may require that entry be made at specific ports in order that such inspection may be made.

The procedure we have followed has been subjected to careful analysis and compared in detail with the language of the Plant Quarantine Act and after mature consideration it is believed that specific authority does not exist for limiting the quantity of nursery stock that may be imported from countries with inspection systems or for designating a given person as one qualified to receive importations or for prescribing the purpose for which a given importation shall be used or for exacting an agreement that the importation shall be grown under departmental observation for a given length of time.

Section 2 of the act requires that a notice shall be given upon arrival of a shipment of nursery stock at the port of entry and that before such stock is removed from the port of entry a notice of shipment shall also be given. No interstate shipment of an importation of nursery stock may be made until either such notice has been given or the stock has been inspected by a State official. Please note that the notice of shipment is to be given before the removal of the importation from the port of entry. This notice is not the condition of entry which a regulation promulgated by the Federal Horticultural Board (HB-134,

March 23, 1921) has attempted to make it. Please also note that, for interstate shipments, a notice of shipment or State inspection is required. Once that notice is given, or as soon as the shipment has received State inspection, further interstate movement is subject only to such restrictions as may apply to interstate movement of like domestic material, except in the matter of marking. Subsequent notices are not required by the act as they are by Quarantine 37.

Section 3 requires that importations of nursery stock are to be marked in a specified manner.

Section 4 requires that importations of nursery stock moving interstate shall be marked in the manner specified unless and until inspected by a State official.

The term "nursery stock," as used in these sections, is defined in section 6 to include "all field-grown florists' stock, trees, shrubs, vines, cuttings, grafts, scions, buds, fruit pits and other seeds of fruit and ornamental trees or shrubs, and other plants and plant products for propagation." Field, vegetable, and flower seeds, bedding plants and other herbaceous plants, bulbs, and roots, are not defined as nursery stock and therefore were not originally subject to the restrictions of entry contained in sections 1 to 4 of the act.

Section 5 provides that whenever the Secretary of Agriculture shall determine that the unrestricted importation of any plant or plant product not defined by the act as nursery stock may result in the entry of injurious pests, he shall call a public hearing and then promulgate his determination, specifying the class of plants or plant products to be restricted and the country or countries where they are grown. Thereafter, or until such promulgation is withdrawn, these materials are enterable only under the conditions laid down in sections 1 to 4, which I have just discussed.

These 5 sections, with the definition of nursery stock in section 6, comprise that part of the Plant Quarantine Act which deals with the restrictions on importations.

Section 7 provides means whereby, after due public hearing, the Secretary of Agriculture may cause the exclusion of a plant or plant product to prevent the introduction of a pest. His determination of such necessity, in the form of a quarantine notice, makes it unlawful to import the plant or plant product for any purpose whatever except by the Department of Agriculture for experimental or scientific purposes. The power of exclusion is in this section of the act itself. The secretary's action in promulgating a notice of quarantine merely makes the act operative with respect to the plant or plant product in question. No provision exists in this section for restricted entry.

With this provision of the act in mind let us look to Quarantine 37 and our method of administering it. At this point it should be stated parenthetically that the classes of plant materials now restricted by that quarantine which are not defined as nursery stock in section 6 of the act, were brought under the provisions of sections 1 to 4 of the act by due process, in accordance with the procedure outlined in section 5. I need say nothing further as to the legal aspects of quantity limits, availability, horticultural qualifications to import, utilization, or delayed release, that is, growing imports under agreement for a period. Nevertheless, Quarantine 37 contains reference to quantity limits and purpose in regulations 1, 3, 4, and 14. Availability is touched upon in regulations 1 and 14. Three definite prohibitions such as should be written in accordance with section 7 of the act, are to be found in regulation 3. These prohibitions are not written into the quarantine itself but are parts of a supplemental regulation. Prohibitions on certain materials have been administered during the past several years under regulations 3, 14, and 15 of Quarantine 37. It is believed these prohibitions should be the subject of prohibitory quarantines under the Plant Quarantine Act or the prohibitions should be dropped.

The foregoing instances indicate that Quarantine 37 should be examined openly in the light of the provisions of the law under which it was promulgated. As previously shown, many steps have already been taken in an effort to bring our administration of this quarantine more nearly into accord with the law.

It is admitted these steps are, not strictly in accordance with the purpose announced when the quarantine was promulgated or with the policies followed in the early years of the administration of that quarantine. The question to be faced squarely is—shall we modify our policies and procedures, and Quarantine 37 to fit the act, or shall the act be modified to fit the policies expressed in and by Quarantine 37? The former step is in our power to take, but the latter is for the Congress to consider. It is my opinion that action in both directions is needed. For example, it would seem proper that we should have legal authority in certain instances to require propagation of imported stock under safeguards until the pest status of the importation has been determined sufficiently to decide whether the risk of introducing pests actually exists. With some shipments it is impossible to make this determination at the time of entry because the immature stages of development of some organisms present are impossible of diagnosis.

Many American growers have built their businesses on the trade protection afforded by the policies followed in administering Quarantine 37. In justice to them the Department has issued repeated statements pointing out that the Plant Quarantine Act and quarantines promulgated thereunder should be administered for the sole purpose of preventing the entry into this country and the spread within the United States of injurious plant pests. These statements have been a warning to growers to adjust their businesses away from the false basis of the trade protection given them by the administrative procedure we have been discussing.

Quarantines are and should be for the purpose of preventing the entry and movement of pests and for facilitating the entry and movement of products. Quarantine 37 has been used more for the purpose of preventing the entry and movement of products and for creating monopolies in the production of certain fancied varieties of plants. At numerous public hearings and conferences held on this quarantine in Washington the evidence has forced one to conclude that the greater interest was in trade protection than in pest protection. We have witnessed not so long ago the spectacle of a certain group urging the continued admission of a large class of products infested by a certain pest on the theory that it had not been proven that this pest would transfer to other commodities. The exclusion was demanded by the same group of another product carrying a pest which cannot be distinguished microscopically from the one infesting the products the entry of which that group demanded. Changes in the quarantine have been made, changes are being made, and changes will continue to be made until finally in spite of the obstacles thrown in the way, the quarantine will be placed on the basis which has for its purpose the prevention of pest movement and not the prevention of plant movement.

In conclusion, I wish to emphasize again the need for more adequate inspection facilities at New York and certain other ports of entry. The examination of plant imports in modern inspection houses in New York and other ports of entry would not only afford greater protection to the country, but would obviate the necessity of shipping plants to Washington, frequently under adverse conditions, not to mention the cost in time and money.

P. Q. C. A. 283, revised, Supplement No. 5.

PLANT-QUARANTINE IMPORT RESTRICTIONS, CUBA

OCTOBER 14, 1937.

STATE CERTIFICATE OF ORIGIN ACCEPTED FOR RICE

Circular No. 81, of August 20, 1937, of the Cuban Direction General of Customs, to attest the origin of rice, granted the benefit of the preferential established in decree No. 2438, August 9, 1937, and prescribed the production of a certificate issued by an association of millers organized prior to the promulgation of that decree and officially recognized by the laws of the United States, and devoted to the industrial handling of rice grown in the United States.

Circular No. 87, of September 8, 1937, amplifies the provisions of Circular No. 81 by prescribing that certificates of origin issued under the seal and signature of State departments of agriculture, affirming that the rice in question is a product of the soil and industry of the United States, will be accepted for rice grown in the United States and exported to Cuba.

LEE A. STRONG,
Chief, Bureau of Entomology and Plant Quarantine.

B. E. P. Q. 368, Supplement No. 2.

PLANT-QUARANTINE IMPORT RESTRICTIONS, REPUBLIC OF POLAND

OCTOBER 14, 1937.

INSPECTION CERTIFICATES REQUIRED IN DUPLICATE

According to the order of the Minister, of Finance, L. D, IV 7953/3/37, of April 1, 1937, the phytosanitary certificate required with each shipment of seeds of clover, alfalfa, sand clover, sweetclover, trefoil, and timothy offered for entry into Poland must be in duplicate. The certificate must conform to the model reproduced in supplement No. 1 to B. E. P. Q.–368 for such seeds.

LEE A. STRONG,
Chief, Bureau of Entomology and Plant Quarantine.

B. E. P, Q. 375, revised, Supplement No. 1.

PLANT-QUARANTINE IMPORT RESTRICTIONS, KINGDOM OF EGYPT

OCTOBER 11, 1937.

PROHIBITING THE IMPORTATION OF CERTAIN FRUITS AND PLANTS WITHOUT IMPORT PERMIT

[Order of the Minister of Agriculture, June 19, 1937]

ARTICLE 1. The order of February 1, 1933, whereby San Jose scale (*Aspidiotus perniciosus* Comst.) was declared injurious to fruit (and which prescribed the fumigation of imported fruits found infested by this pest), is revoked.

ART. 2. Article 2 of the order of August 30, 1933, which prohibited the importation into Egypt of fruits and plants without the permission of the Minister of Agriculture, is amended as follows:

IMPORTATION OF ADDITIONAL PLANTS AND FRUITS PROHIBITED

"ART. 2.—Paragraph (1) of article 2 of law No. 1 of 1916 is supplemented as follows:
"(*a*) Plants, parts of plants, and fruits of the following families: Coniferae (Pinaceae, Taxaceae), Cupuliferae (Betulaceae and Fagaceae). Juglandaceae, Moraceae, Papilionaceae (Leguminoseae), Rosaceae, Rutaceae, Salicaceae, Solanaceae, Tiliaceae, Vitaceae.
"(*b*) Kaki fruit (*Diospyros kaki* L.).
"(*c*) Onions.
"(*d*) All plants in pots or with balls of earth or sand."

IMPORTATION PROHIBITED OF PLANTS AND FRUITS ATTACKED BY SAN JOSE SCALE

ART. 3. Article 3 of the order of August 30, 1933 (which declared *Pseudococcus* spp. as insects injurious to fruits and prescribed that any imported fruits infested with those pests must be fumigated) receives the following new paragraphs:
"The insect *Aspidiotus perniciosus* Comst. is declared injurious to fruits and plants.
"The importation into Egypt of all fruits, plants, and parts of plants infested with this insect is prohibited."
Consequently the following item should be added to the summary of B. E. P. Q. 375, revised, under the caption "Importation Prohibited":
Fruits, plants, and parts of plants; Importation into Egypt prohibited if infested with San Jose scale (*Aspidiotus perniciosus* Comst.). (Order of June 19, 1937, art. 3.)

LEE A. STRONG,
Chief, Bureau of Entomology and Plant Quarantine.

B. E. P. Q. 380, revised.

PLANT-QUARANTINE IMPORT RESTRICTIONS, REPUBLIC OF HAITI

OCTOBER 14, 1937.

This revision of the digest of the plant-quarantine import restrictions of the Republic of Haiti has been prepared for the information of nurserymen, plant-quarantine officials, and others interested in the exportation of plants and plant products to that country. It became necessary because the order of July 24, 1937, superseded that of November 23, 1934.

It was prepared by Harry B. Shaw, plant quarantine inspector, in charge of Foreign Information Service of the Division of Foreign Plant Quarantines, from his translations of the texts of the law of August 2, 1934, and the order of July 24, 1937, and reviewed by the Service National de la Production Agricole et de l'Enseignement Rural of Haiti.

The information contained in this circular is believed to be correct and complete up to the time of preparation, but it is not intended to be used independently of, nor as a substitute for, the original texts, and it is not to be interpreted as legally authoritative.

LEE A. STRONG,
Chief, Bureau of Entomology and Plant Quarantine.

PLANT-QUARANTINE IMPORT RESTRICTIONS, REPUBLIC OF HAITI

BASIC LEGISLATION

The law of August 2, 1934, empowers the President to establish by order all necessary regulations to prevent the entry into the Republic of insects, pathogenic organisms, and agents that transmit plant and animal diseases, and to combat diseases that may prejudice plant or animal production, as well as to impose penalties for violations of the provisions of such regulations.

GENERAL REGULATIONS

[Order of July 24, 1937]

IMPORTATION PROHIBITED

ARTICLE 1. The importation of the field-crop plants hereafter named, or of parts of those plants (roots, stems, cuttings, fruits, seeds, etc.) into Haiti, is prohibited, even when accompanied by a phytosanitary certificate, namely, coffee (*Coffea* spp.), cotton (*Gossypium* spp.), sugarcane (*Saccharum officinarum* L.), coconut palms (*Cocos nucifera* L.) *Citrus*, banana (*Musa* spp.), cacao (*Theobroma cacao* L.), and sisal (*Agave sisalana* Perrine), as well as any other plant that may later be designated by the Service National de la Production Agricole et de l'Enseignement Rural (National Service of Agricultural Production and Rural Education).

However, that service may exceptionally introduce the above-named plants or parts thereof for technical or economic purposes on taking necessary precautions to protect the agriculture of Haiti against the introduction of injurious insects or diseases.

COMMERCIAL SAMPLES MAY ENTER SUBJECT TO INSPECTION ON ARRIVAL

The said service may also authorize certain exporters to receive commercial samples of coffee, cacao, citrus, coconuts, and fig-bananas from their foreign correspondents, provided that such samples have been previously inspected by a qualified agent of the said service and found free from injurious insects and plant diseases.

PASSENGERS MUST DECLARE PLANTS IN BAGGAGE

ART. 2. Passengers landing in Haiti will be required to make a statement in their customs declarations of the presence of any plant or part thereof, such as roots, stems, cuttings, fruits, seeds, etc., and especially of coffee plants in their baggage.

CERTIFICATION OF FRESH FRUITS AGAINST MEDITERRANEAN FRUITFLY

ART. 3. Fresh fruits intended for consumption may be imported on condition that they are accompanied by a certificate affirming that they have been sterilized or that they proceed from a region in which the Mediterranean fruitfly (*Ceratitis capitata* Wied.). does not exist. The certificate should be signed by a qualified agent of the government of the country of origin.

In default of such a certificate, the fruits and their packing will be destroyed without delay under the supervision of the customs authorities.

ART. 4. Fresh fruits grown in certain countries, such as the United States of America, Canada, Jamaica, Puerto Rico, etc., will be beneficiaries of the privilege granted by paragraph 2 of article 5 to ornamentals and vegetables (truck crops), provided that their origin is certified by competent authorities of the said countries and that they arrive in vessels that have not touched at ports of countries reputed to be contaminated.

CERTIFICATION OF ORNAMENTALS AND VEGETABLES REQUIRED

ART. 5. Plant species known as ornamentals or vegetables, including slips, cuttings, or any part other than seeds, entering Haiti, should be accompanied by a phytosanitary certificate signed by a qualified agent of the government of the country of origin, attesting that the said plants or parts thereof are free from infectious diseases and injurious insects or that they do not proceed from fields infested by such insects and diseases.

In default of a phytosanitary certificate, plants or parts thereof and their packing will be destroyed without delay under supervision of customs authorities. Exceptionally, however, such plants or parts of plants imported through Port-au-Prince may be forwarded to destination after inspection by a qualified agent of the S. N. P. A. and E. R. and the obligatory issuance of a certificate in proper form.

ART. 6. The following fresh products: Tomatoes, peppers, green beans, melons, cucumbers, and pumpkins imported from countries other than those named in article 4 should be accompanied by the certificate prescribed by article 3, otherwise they will be destroyed without delay, together with their packing, under customs supervision.

ART. 7. The expenses involved by the inspection provided in article 5, including the traveling expenses of the agent of the S. N. P. A. and E. R., will be charged to the consignee and must be paid by him before the issuance of the certificate, in accordance with the established tariff.

CERTIFICATION OF CEREALS AND DRIED OR PRESERVED FRUITS NOT REQUIRED

ART. 8. Cereals such as corn (*Zea mays* L.), wheat, rice, oats, barley; dried vegetables, vegetable seeds, and flowers; dried or preserved fruits, such as grapes, peaches, plums, candied fruit, etc., do not fall under the restrictions of the present order and may be imported into Haiti without phytosanitary certificate.

FREE INSPECTION SERVICE AT PORT-AU-PRINCE

ART. 9. A regular free inspection service has been established at Port-au-Prince by the S. N. P. A. and E. R. to proceed, once a week, to inspect plant products entering that port.

ART. 10. In all cases not provided for in the preceding articles, the customs will consult the S. N. P. A. and E. R. before finally delivering products to their consignees.

CERTIFICATION FOR EXPORT

ART. 11. Qualified agents of the S. N. P. A. and E. R. alone, on exportation, may issue the certificates required by foreign countries for the importation of plant or animal products of Haiti.

ART. 12. The present order revokes that of November 23, 1934.

B. E. P. Q. 420, Supplement No. 1.

PLANT-QUARANTINE IMPORT RESTRICTIONS, REPUBLIC OF FINLAND

OCTOBER 14, 1937.

REGULATIONS GOVERNING THE IMPORTATION OF SEEDS

[Decree No. 149, April 9, 1937; Finlands Författningssamling, April 10, 1937]

Decree No. 149 revokes and supersedes that of March 9, 1920 (p. 7 et seq., B. E. P. Q. 420). The following regulations are now effective:

ARTICLE 1. The Agricultural Administration, in case of necessity, on the suggestion of the Government Seed Control Station, must make proposals to the

Ministry of Agriculture on seeds whose importation into and exportation from Finland are to be prohibited or restricted.

Articles 2 and 3 pertain to entry procedure.

SAMPLES TO BE TAKEN FOR ANALYSIS

ART. 4. Whoever intends to sell, to import into Finland, or to export from Finland seeds that are restricted by a decision of the Ministry of Agriculture, must withdraw samples of them in the prescribed manner and send them to the Seed Control Institute for examination.

UNFIT SEEDS TO BE REEXPORTED

ART. 5. Seeds which, on the examination mentioned in article 3, are found unfit for introduction into commerce must be sent abroad again within 3 months of their entry into Finland, if the Ministry of Agriculture does not otherwise order.

CLOVER AND PLANT SEEDS MUST BE COLORED

ART. 6. Seeds of clover (*Trifolium*), alfalfa (*Medicago*), sand clover (*Anthyllis*), sweetclover (*Melilotus*), trefoil (*Lotus*), and seeds of all species of plants whose origin, in the opinion of the Ministry of Agriculture, is of significance to the welfare of crops, must be stained with a solution of eosin before being introduced into commerce.

Staining must be effected by injecting red coloring matter (eosin) dissolved in denatured alcohol in several places in each sack. The strength of the eosin solution must be 0.8 percent (8 gm of eosin to 1 liter of denatured alcohol).

Articles 7 and 8 provide for the annual publication of the minimal requirements concerning purity, germinability, and content of weed seeds and for the determination of the selling period.

CONTAINERS MUST BE MARKED "FOREIGN SEEDS"

ART. 9. Imported seeds whose origin, in the opinion of the Department of Agriculture, is of significance to the welfare of crops, must be provided with containers on which the words "Utlandskt frö" (foreign seeds) are clearly and permanently marked.

LEE A. STRONG,
Chief, Bureau of Entomology and Plant Quarantine.

B. E. P. Q. 426, Supplement No. 2.

PLANT-QUARANTINE IMPORT RESTRICTIONS, REPUBLIC OF ARGENTINA

November 2, 1937.

AMENDED REGULATIONS GOVERNING IMPORTATION OF POTATOES

[Decree No. 115748 of October 4, 1937]

ARTICLE 1. Articles 55 to 59 of decree No. 83732 of June 3, 1936, promulgating regulations under law No. 4084 (see pp. 21 and 22, B. E. P. Q. 426) are amended to read as follows:

"CERTIFICATION OF POTATOES

"ART. 55. Every shipment of potatoes introduced into Argentina, besides meeting the general conditions established by these regulations, shall be accompanied by the following certificates:

"Seed potatoes: Certificate of healthy origin and phytosanitary shipping certificate (inspection certificate). In the first, it is necessary to affirm, besides what is prescribed in article 8, that the crops from which the tubers proceed are found free from potato wart (*Synchytrium endobioticum* (Schilb.) Perc.); potato tuber worm (*Gnorimoschema operculella* Zell.); Colorado potato beetle (*Leptinotarsa decemlineata* Say); and 'virus diseases', allowing a tolerance up to 2 percent for the last.

"Potatoes for consumption: Phytosanitary shipping certificate.

"Art. 56. Shipments of such potatoes shall meet the following conditions: (a) (1) They shall be well formed; (2) clean; (3) free from tubers having mechanical lesions or those caused by insects or other means; (4) free from internal changes of whatever origin; (5) tubers exposed to the sun, flaccid ones; (6) sprouted tubers; (7) scabby potatoes; (8) tubers with dry spots or rots; and (9) must be free from any serious disease or parasite that does not occur in Argentina.

"(b) Judgment of defects, lesions, or diseases referred to in paragraph (a) will be made by taking into account their intensity and seriousness and their effect upon the general appearance of the tubers in accordance with the following criteria:

"(1) Good shape: When the appearance of each tuber, or the general appearance, is not marred by excessively pointed or constricted tubers or those with secondary growths or excrescences;

"(2) Cleanliness: When the general appearance of the tubers is not obviously affected by soil or dirt of any kind;

"(3) Tubers that are bruised, cut, cracked, punctured, etc., to such an extent that the lesions manifestly injure each tuber;

"(4) Hollow heart, black heart, or any abnormal discoloration of the tuber;

"(5) Tubers that are old and clearly found to be soft and spongy;

"(6) Sprouted tubers; when more than 10 percent have sprouts exceeding 1.5 cm in length;

"(7) Tubers attacked by common scab (*Actinomyces scabies* (Thax.) Guss.), black scab (*Rhizoctonia solani* Kuhn), etc., to such an extent that the lesions seriously affect the tuber;

"(8) Any decomposition of tubers, total or partial, due to any cause whatever;

"(9) *Synchytrium endobioticum, Gnorimoschema operculella*, etc.

TOLERANCES

"(c) Within the criteria set forth in the preceding paragraphs, a tolerance is allowed of 5 percent in seed potatoes and 10 percent in potatoes for consumption in the aggregate of defects, lesions, and common diseases. Among those percentages, only 1 percent of tubers affected by rot may be included, no tolerance being allowed for diseases and pests that do not occur in Argentina.

"(d) The percentages of tolerance are calculated in the following manner: A determined number of packages is inspected in each shipment, and the percentage of tubers attacked is ascertained in each of them by weight; those percentages having been obtained, the average is calculated and applied to the whole shipment as the basis of tolerance.

"(e) Shipments that exceed the tolerances established in paragraph (c) will be subject to selection (culling) or to disinfection, as the respective sanitary authorities may decide, charging the expenses thus arising to the account of the interested person. Shipments found to be attacked by dangerous diseases or pests that do not occur in Argentina will be reladen or destroyed, in accordance with the provisions of article 5, the cost thereof being charged to the account of the interested person.

CONDITIONS UNDER WHICH SEED POTATOES MAY BE IMPORTED

"Art. 57. Tubers intended for planting must meet the following conditions:

"(a) The importation of 'certified' potatoes only will be permitted; that is, they must proceed from crops recorded by the special seed-potato certifying services, crops that are subject to supervision by preestablished agencies of the National or State governments or of official experiment stations of the countries of origin;

"(b) The potatoes shall arrive in cases weighing 50 kg net, having a partition in the middle, each case bearing a certification tag (or ticket) approved by the official service that issued it. Each tag will state that the seed potatoes are 'certified' and indicate also the name of the grower, the variety, and the place of origin;

"(c) The minimal weight of potatoes intended for planting shall be 40 gm with a tolerance up to 5 percent in the weight of smaller tubers.

CONDITIONS UNDER WHICH POTATOES FOR CONSUMPTION MAY BE IMPORTED

"ART. 58. Tubers intended for consumption shall meet the following conditions:

"(a) They shall come in containers not exceeding 60 kg net weight, each bearing the printed inscription 'PAPAS PARA CONSUMO' (potatoes for consumption) in quite legible characters, as well as the name of the variety.

"(b) The weight of the tubers shall not be less than 60 gm, a tolerance up to 5 percent by weight of smaller potatoes being allowed.

AUTHORIZED PORTS OF ENTRY FOR POTATOES

"ART. 59. Potatoes may be imported only through the ports of Buenos Aires and Rio Gallegos."

NOTE: In the absence of definite information concerning potato diseases and insect pests that do not occur in Argentina, inspectors should be guided by the list furnished in the original article 56, page 21 of B. E. P. Q. 426.

LEE A. STRONG,
Chief, Bureau of Entomology and Plant Quarantine.

B. E. P. Q. 429, Supplement No. 1.

PLANT-QUARANTINE IMPORT RESTRICTIONS, NETHERLANDS EAST INDIES

NOVEMBER 9, 1937.

DECREE No. 9760–A. Z., NOVEMBER 3, 1926, AMENDED

The general regulations promulgated under decree No. 9760–A. Z., of November 3, 1926, have again been amended by decree No. 18239–A. Z., of December 28, 1936, and decree No. 8459, of June 9, 1937, as follows:

SECTION IV (a) AMENDED

. The following items are to be stricken from the list of vegetables, herbs, fruits, and medicinal plants in section IV (a) (p. 5 of B. E. P. Q. 429):

Allium spp., chive, garlic, leek, onion, shallot, etc.
Brassica spp., broccoli, cabbage, cauliflower, kale, kohlrabi, mustard, pe-tsai, pak-tsoi, rutabaga, turnip, etc.
Cochlearia officinalis, scurvygrass.
Daucus carota, carrot.
Lepidium sativum, peppergrass, cress.
Radicula armoracia, horseradish.
Radicula-nasturtium-aquaticum, watercress.
Raphanus sativus, radish.
Sinapis.
Sisymbrium.

The names of the following ornamentals are to be stricken from section IV (b) (p. 6, B. E. P. Q. 429):

Cheiranthus, Iberis, Lunaria, and *Matthiola.*

The name "*Agaricus*" is to be replaced by "*Psalliota*" in section IV (e), (p. 7, B. E. P. Q. 429):

DISINFECTION OF CERTAIN SEEDS REQUIRED

The following new article (2a) is to be inserted between articles 2 and 3 of section V of decree No. 9760–A. Z., of November 3, 1926, as amended (p. 8, B. E. P. Q. 429):

ARTICLE 2a. With respect to the seeds of *Allium* spp., chive, garlic, leek, onion, shallot, etc.; *Apium graveolens*, celery; *Brassica* spp., broccoli, cabbage, cauliflower, kale, kohlrabi, mustard, pak-tsoi, pe-tsai, rutabaga, turnip, etc.; *Cheiranthus,* wallflower; *Cochlearia,* scurvygrass; *Cucurbits,* cucumber, melon, etc.; *Daucus,* carrot; *Gossypium,* cotton; *Iberis,* candytuft; *Lepidium,* cress, peppergrass; *Lunaria,* honesty; *Matthiola,* stocks; *Medicago,* alfalfa; *Melilotus,* sweetclover; (*Nasturtium*) *Radicula-nasturtium-aquaticum; Onobrychis,* sainfoin; *Radicula armoracia,* horseradish; *Raphanus,* radish; *Sinapis*—see *Brassica*;

Sisymbrium—see *Radicula-nasturtium-aquaticum;* and *Trifolium*, clover, with-. out prejudice to the applicability of the other provisions of this decree, the importation into the Netherlands East Indies of the above-named seeds and the packing material in which they were shipped is not permitted until they have been disinfected in accordance with the provisions of sections II and III. (Sections II and III authorize the designation of inspectors of plants and of fresh fruits, respectively, at authorized ports of entry.)

The provision in the first paragraph of this article does not apply with respect to shipments of seeds of the plants named in that paragraph, except cotton, if the declaration is made in the phytosanitary certificate issued by the phytopathological service at Wageningen, that the seeds have been disin- fected in a disinfection plant operating under the supervision of the service.

AVERY S. HOYT,
Acting Chief, Bureau of Entomology and Plant Quarantine.

B. P. Q. 350, Supplement No. 2.

PLANT-QUARANTINE IMPORT RESTRICTIONS, KINGDOM OF NORWAY

OCTOBER 26, 1937.

IMPORTATION PROHIBITED OF PLANTS FROM THE UNITED STATES AND CERTAIN OTHER COUNTRIES

[Royal decree of September 24, 1937—Effective immediately]

ARTICLE 1. In conformity with the law of July 21, 1926, Section 2 (*a*) con- cerning the suppression of injurious insects and plant diseases, the importation into Norway of living plants with roots, as well as roots, rhizomes, tubers, bulbs, tomatoes, and eggplants from the United States of America, Canada, France, Belgium, and Luxemburg is prohibited to prevent the introduction of the Colorado potato beetle (*Leptinotarsa decemlineata* Say).

ART. 2. The Norwegian Department of Agriculture (Landbruksdepartementet) is authorized to dispense with the above regulation under conditions stipulated by that Department.

AVERY S. HOYT,
Acting Chief, Bureau of Entomology and Plant Quarantine.

B. E. P. Q. 433, Supplement No. 1.

PLANT-QUARANTINE IMPORT RESTRICTIONS, COLONY OF BARBADOS, BRITISH WEST INDIES

OCTOBER 11, 1937.

COTTON RESTRICTIONS EXTENDED

An amendment dated August 7, 1937, has been made to the Cotton Diseases Prevention Act of 1928, in consequence of which the following item should be substituted for the first item on page 2 of B. E. P. Q. 433:

Cottonseed, seed cotton, lint, *or part of the cotton plant, or any other plant belonging to the family Malvaceae, or any article stuffed with or containing any of the same:* May be imported only by permission of the Governor-in- Executive-Committee. (Cotton Diseases Prevention [Amendment] Act, August 7, 1937.)

LEE A. STRONG,
Chief, Bureau of Entomology and Plant Quarantine.

B. E. P. Q. 434, Revised.

PLANT-QUARANTINE IMPORT RESTRICTIONS, COLONY OF ST. LUCIA, BRITISH WEST INDIES

OCTOBER 14, 1937.

This revision of the digest of the plant-quarantine import restrictions of the Colony of St. Lucia has been prepared for the information of nurserymen, plant-quarantine officials, and others interested in the exportation of plants and plant products to that Colony.

This revision was rendered necessary by the promulgation of the customs (Importation of Fruit from the United States of America) notice of September 7, 1937, and proclamation No. 33 of August 21, 1937.

It was prepared by Harry B. Shaw, plant quarantine inspector in charge, Foreign Information Service, Division of Foreign Plant Quarantines, from the original texts of the ordinances and proclamations of the Governor in Council, and reviewed by the agricultural superintendent of the Colony.

The information contained in this circular is believed to be correct and complete up to the time of preparation, but it is not intended to be used independently of, nor as a substitute for, the original texts, and it is not to be interpreted as legally authoritative. The original ordinances and proclamations should be consulted for the exact texts.

LEE A. STRONG,
Chief, Bureau of Entomology and Plant Quarantine.

PLANT-QUARANTINE IMPORT RESTRICTIONS, COLONY OF ST. LUCIA, BRITISH WEST INDIES

BASIC LEGISLATION

[Plants Protection Ordinances, 1909 and 1913, as revised by No. 14 of 1916]

Under these ordinances, the Governor in Council may, by proclamation, absolutely or conditionally prohibit the importation, directly or indirectly, from any country or place, of plants, or earth or soil, or any article packed therewith, or packages or other articles or things which in the opinion of the Governor in Council are or is likely to be a means of introducing any plant disease or pest into the Colony.

DEFINITION OF PLANT

"Plant" includes tree, shrub, herb, or vegetable; and cuttings, bulbs, seeds, berries, buds, and grafts; and the fruit or other product of any plant; and the whole or any part of any growing, dying, or dead plant, including emptied pods, husks, or skins.

SUMMARY

IMPORTATION PROHIBITED

Plants and seeds of all kinds from Ceylon: General precautions to prevent the introduction of injurious plant diseases or pests. (Proclamation No. 14 of 1916, chap. 7, art. 2 (*a*).)

Cocoa plants (*Theobroma cacao* L.) or parts thereof from South America east and south of the Isthmus of Panama: General precautions to prevent the introduction of injurious diseases and pests. (Proc. No. 14 of 1916, chap. 7, art. 2 (*b*).)

Banana plants (*Musa* spp.), suckers, or parts thereof, from Grenada, Jamaica, Trinidad, Tobago, or any part of Central America or South America: General precautions to prevent the introduction of injurious plant diseases and pests. (Proc. No. 14 of 1916, chap. 7, art. 2 (*c*), as amended by the proc. gazetted September 8, 1917, and that gazetted May 23, 1925.)

Bananas, banana plants, or parts thereof (*Musa* spp.) from the Canary Islands or West Africa: General precautions to prevent the introduction of injurious plant diseases and pests. (Proc. gazetted December 29, 1925.)

Coconuts (*Cocos nucifera* L.), coconut plants, or parts thereof from any country or place, to prevent the introduction of the "red ring disease" (*Aphelenchoides cocophilus* (Cobb) Goodey). (Proc. No. 14 of 1916, chap. 7, art. 2, superseded by the proc. gazetted April 12, 1924.)

Citrus plants (including all plants of the tribe Citratae), or parts thereof, and citrus fruits and parts thereof from any place outside of the Colony, to prevent the introduction of citrus canker (*Bacterium citri* (Hasse) Doidge). (Proc. No. 14 of 1916, chap. 7, art. 2 (*e*), as amended by that gazetted March 26, 1927.)

Earth or soil with plants or parts thereof, to prevent the introduction of injurious plant parasites. (Proc. No. 14 of 1916, chap. 7, art. 2 (*f*).)

Coffee, guava, mango, sapodilla, and star apples, to prevent the introduction of the citrus black fly (*Aleurocanthus woglumi* Ashby) : Importation prohibited of plants, cuttings, fruits, or parts thereof, from Bahamas, Ceylon, Cuba, India, Jamaica, and the Philippines.   (Proc. gazetted February 10, 1917.)

Cottonseed or seed cotton (*Gossypium* spp.) : Importation from any country or place prohibited to prevent the introduction of the pink bollworm (*Pectinophora gossypiella* Saund.).   (Proc. gazetted April 12, 1924.)

Cottonseed products: Proclamation No. 33, of August 21, 1937, of the Governor in Council, prohibits the importation into the Colony of St. Lucia of the following articles from Cuba, Haiti, Mexico, Santo Domingo, United States of America, and parts of Central America as far south as Costa Rica, namely :

(*a*) Cottonseed cake and meal and other cottonseed products, cotton lint, and any part of the cotton plant.

(*b*) Any other malvaceous plants or parts thereof, such as okra, musk okra, or hibiscus seed.

(*c*) Fertilizers and stock feeds containing cottonseed meal.

(*d*) All agricultural produce in bags.

(*e*) Baling material.

(*f*) Any other container that has contained any of the articles listed in (*a*) and (*b*).

(*g*) Any articles that have formed part of the cargo of a ship, another part of the cargo of which has been declared by the inspection officer to be infected or is suspected of being infected.

(*h*) Personal baggage or effects of any description that have been in contact with or in close proximity to other baggage, cargo, or articles of any description infected or suspected of being infected.

Vegetables (except onions, potatoes, and canned or processed vegetables) from all countries other than the British Isles, Canada, British West Indies (except Bahamas, Bermuda, and British Guiana) ; fruits (expect plantains, nuts, dried, canned, candied, and other processed fruits) from all countries other than the British Isles, Canada, British West Indies (except Bahamas, Bermuda, and British Guiana), and the United States of America.   (Proc. gazetted November 29, 1930, as amended by the customs notice of September 7, 1937.)

IMPORTATION RESTRICTED

Sugarcane plants (*Saccharum officinarum* L.), cuttings, or parts thereof, grass, fodder, seeds of grasses and sorghum from any place beyond the limits of the Colony, to prevent the introduction of the mosaic or yellow mottling disease: Importation prohibited except under license from the Governor.   (Proc. gazetted April 2, 1921.)

Vegetables (except onions, potatoes, and canned or processed vegetables) from the British Isles, Canada, British West Indies (except Bahamas, Bermuda, and British Guiana) ; fruits from the same countries and from the United States of America : Must be accompanied by a certificate, issued by the Department of Agriculture of the place of origin, indicating origin and certifying the freedom of the product and the area where grown from the Mediterranean fruitfly.   (Proc. gazetted November 29, 1930, as amended by customs notice of September 7, 1927.)

Plants and parts of plants, other than those whose entry is prohibited, may be imported through the port of Castries, subject to immediate delivery to the agricultural authority for conveyance to the disinfecting plant for such treatment as he may deem fit.   (Proc. No. 14 of 1926, art. 4.)

IMPORTATION UNRESTRICTED

Onions, potatoes, canned or processed vegetables, plantains, nuts, dried, canned, candied, and processed fruits: May be imported without permit or phytosanitary certificate.   (Proc. of November 29, 1930.)

Plants for scientific purposes: The Governor may allow the importation of plants for scientific purposes without their being subject to fumigation, on the application of the Imperial Commissioner of Agriculture or of the agricultural authority.   (Proc. No. 14 of 1916, art. 5.)

B. E. P. Q. 444, Supplement No. 1.

PLANT-QUARANTINE IMPORT RESTRICTIONS, FRENCH ZONE OF MOROCCO

OCTOBER 14 1937.

[Order of August 1, 1936, amended by that of January 23, 1937]

The following paragraphs are added to article 4 of the order of August 1, 1936. (See pp. 18 and 19, B. E. P. Q. 444.)

"Shipments of potatoes covered by paragraphs (a), (b), or (c) of this article must be accompanied by a certificate in the prescribed form (see art. 2, pp. 17 and 18, for the English text and model 2 on p. 23 for the French text). This certificate must also affirm that in the locality of the signatory officials, and in accordance with the existing provisions, the tubers have been cleaned and packed in new containers. (See certificate model 3, pp. 20, 23, and 24.) The containers must be marked to identify the shipment."

"PROVISIONS APPLICABLE ALSO TO TOMATOES AND EGGPLANTS

"The provisions of this article, with the exception of those applying to cleaning, apply also to tomatoes and eggplants:

"(a) That originate in land within the territory of countries infested by the Colorado potato beetle;

"(b) That are in transit and were shipped by routes other than by sea through such countries, or

"(c) That originate in land lying within the boundary of a country contiguous to infested ones and when the Colorado potato beetle has not been determined within 50 km of its boundary.

"Shipments of potatoes, tomatoes, and eggplants covered by paragraphs (a), (b), and (c), above, will be permitted entry only when the governments of the countries concerned have transmitted the names and signatures of the officials assigned to ports for the previously described supervision, together with a specimen of the seal."

The first paragraph of article 5 is amended to read as follows:

"ART. 5. Transshipment in a port of a country infested by the Colorado potato beetle is not regarded as transit when the consignments are forwarded to that port by sea and when the consular authority representing the country of origin at the port of transshipment declares the merchandise to have been transshipped directly from ship to ship."

LEE A. STRONG,
Chief, Bureau of Entomology and Plant Quarantine.

B. E. P. Q. 447, Supplement No. 2.

PLANT-QUARANTINE IMPORT RESTRICTIONS, KINGDOM OF YUGOSLAVIA

OCTOBER 14, 1937.

IMPORTATION OF SEEDLINGS OF DOUGLAS FIR PROHIBITED

The order of the Minister of Agriculture of Yugoslavia, No. 85834/36, of January 13, 1937 (Sluzbene Novine No. 23, February 2, 1937), prohibits the importation of seedlings of Douglas fir (*Pseudotsuga douglasi* Carr.) into Yugoslavia to prevent the introduction of the needle cast disease (*Rhabdocline pseudotsugae* Syd.).

Until further notice, the importation of the seeds of Douglas fir is unrestricted, since the needle cast disease is not seed-borne.

LEE A. STRONG,
Chief, Bureau of Entomology and Plant Quarantine.

B. E. P. Q. 465, Superseding B. E. P. Q. 398.

PLANT-QUARANTINE IMPORT RESTRICTIONS, FRENCH COLONIES

OCTOBER 14, 1937.

This digest of the plant-quarantine import restrictions of French Colonies has been prepared for the information of nurserymen, plant-quarantine officials, and others interested in the exportation of plants and plant products to those colonies.

It was prepared by Harry B. Shaw, plant quarantine inspector in charge, Foreign Information Service, Division of Foreign Plant Quarantines, from the original texts of the pertinent decrees and orders of the French Minister of Colonies and of the respective Colonies, and reviewed by the French Ministry of Colonies.

The information contained in this circular is believed to be correct and complete up to the time of preparation, but it is not intended to be used independently of, nor as a substitute for, the original texts of the decrees and orders concerned. They should be consulted for the exact texts.

LEE A. STRONG,
Chief, Bureau of Entomology and Plant Quarantine.

PLANT-QUARANTINE IMPORT RESTRICTIONS, FRENCH COLONIES

(Including Cameroons, Equatorial Africa, Guadeloupe and Dependencies, Guiana, India (Settlements in), Indo-China, Madagascar and Dependencies, Martinique, New Caledonia and Dependencies, New Hebrides, Oceania (Settlements in), Reunion Island, Somaliland, Togoland, West Africa)

BASIC LEGISLATION

[Decree of May 6, 1913, to prevent the introduction of coffee rust (*Hemileia vastatrix* B. and Br.) and other pests and diseases]

Article 1 of this decree, in order to prevent the distribution of plant diseases caused by animal or plant parasites or by larvae or nonparasitic insects, empowers the Minister of Colonies, through special orders that name the disease and the plants susceptible to infection, to prohibit the entry into the French Colonies and Protectorates, other than Algeria, Morocco, and Tunisia, of—

1. Plants susceptible to the declared disease;
2. All other plants whereby that disease could be transported;
3. Soils or composts that may contain parasites, larvae, or nonparasitic insects in any stage of development.

The same article prescribes that Governors-General or Governors, by order, shall determine plants, soils, or composts which are capable of carrying the disease, and prescribes that the importation of the containers or packing of such materials may also be prohibited.

Article 2 prescribes that the Minister of Colonies may, in default of a prohibition, determine through a special order the conditions to which the entry and distribution of the plants and articles mentioned shall be subject in the colonies and protectorates, and the conditions under which branches, leaves, fruits, seeds, and refuse of the said plants may enter into and move within the said colonies and protectorates.

PLANTS AFFECTED BY IMPORT RESTRICTIONS OF THE FRENCH COLONIES

General orders have been issued by the French Minister of Colonies to impose restrictions upon or prohibitions against the importation of certain plants and plant products into all French colonies, or groups of French colonies. From time to time these general orders have been applied to particular colonies by special or local orders promulgated by the respective Governors-General or Governors of the colonies concerned.

The plants hitherto affected by these orders are: Banana (*Musa* spp.), cocoa (*Theobroma cacao* L.), coconut palm (*Cocos nucifera* L.), coffee (*Coffea* spp.), cotton (*Gossypium* spp.), rubber (*Hevea* spp.), sugarcane (*Saccharum officinarum* L.), tea (*Thea* spp.), fruits (applied to Indo-China only), potatoes (*Solanum tuberosum* L.) (applied to New Caledonia only), and trees, cuttings, roots, seeds, bulbs (applied to New Caledonia only).

The prohibitions and restrictions are applicable to the above-mentioned plants proceeding from the sources named in the respective orders, which should be consulted.

Consequently, the importation of other plants and plant products into the French colonies is not restricted, except in the cases of Indo-China, New Caledonia, and Oceania.

Special orders have been promulgated to ·control the importation of plants and plant products into Indo-China and New Caledonia.

The ·import restrictions and prohibitions are summarized under each colony separately, with references to the respective local and general orders; the latter should be consulted· for full particulars.

CAMEROONS

Banana plants (*Musa* spp.) : See .orders of February 11, 1931, and February 9, 1935, applying the order of December 7, 1926, page 25.

Coffee (*Coffea* spp.) :. Domestic restrictions only.

Cotton (*Gossypium* spp.) : See order of February 22, 1926, page 32.

Sugarcane (*Saccharum officinarum* L.) : See order of December 3, 1929, page 34.

EQUATORIAL AFRICA

(Including Gabon, Middle Congo, Oubangi-Chari, Tchad)

Banana plants (*Musa* spp.) : See orders of February 11, 1931, and February 9, 1935, applying the order of December 7, 1926, page 25.

.Cocoa plants (*Theobroma cacao* L.) .: See order of December 3, 1929, page 26.

Coffee ·plants (*Coffea* spp.), berries, or seeds, and any plant· capable of distributing coffee rust (*Hemileia vastatrix* B. and Br.) : See order of May 19, 1924, page 30.

Sugarcane (*Saccharum officinarum* L.) : See order of December 3, 1929, page 34.

GUIANA

Banana plants (*Musa* spp.) : See order of February 9, 1935, applying the order of December 7, 1926, page 25.

Cocoa plants (*Theobroma cacoa* L.) : See order of December ·3, 1929, page 26.

Coffee plants (*Coffea* spp.), berries, or seeds: See order of May 19, 1924, to prevent the introduction of coffee rust (*Hemileia vastatrix* B. and Br.), page 30.

Coffee plants (*Coffea* spp.), and parts thereof, dry or fresh beans, beans in parchment, hulled beans (fresh or unroasted), soil and composts, containers, and plants capable of harboring the coffee-berry borer (*Stephanoderes hampei* Hag.), especially *Hibiscus* and *Rubus*: See order of February 27, 1922, page 28.

Cotton (*Gossypium* spp.), plants or parts thereof in the dry or green state, ginned or unginned cotton, cottonseed, soil or compost, packing or containers, and seeds, plants, etc., capable of harboring the pink bollworm, especially *Hibiscus cannabinus, H. esculentus*, and *Bauhinia*: See order of February 26, 1926, page 32.

Sugarcane (*Saccharum officinarum* L.) : See order of December 3, 1929, page 34.

INDIA, SETTLEMENTS IN

(Including Chendernagore, Karikal, Mahe, Pondichery, and Yanaon)

Banana plants: No restrictions.

Coconut (*Cocos nucifera* L.) palms, nuts, and leaves, and any material capable of harboring parasites that attack the coconut palm: See order of August 1, 1927, below.

Cotton (*Gossypium* spp.) : See order of February 22, 1926, page 32.

Sugarcane (*Saccharum officinarum* L.) : See order of December 3, 1929, page 34.

IMPORTATION OF COCONUT PALMS, NUTS, AND LEAVES PROHIBITED

[Ministerial order of August 1, 1927]

ARTICLE 1. The importation by sea, the distribution, storage, and transit of coconut palms, coconuts, and leaves of the coconut palm, and of any other material that may contain parasites that attack this palm are prohibited for the French Settlements of India and Oceania.

INDO-CHINA

(Including Annam, Cambodia, Cochin-China, Laos, and Tonkin)

Separate orders have been promulgated to control the importation of plants and plant products into Indo-China. A summary of those orders follows:

Banana (*Musa* spp.): The importation, distribution, storage, and transit are prohibited of entire plants or parts thereof, fruits, and seeds of all species of banana, and of soil and packing accompanying them, provided that they may be imported from a country declared not infected by the Panama wilt disease (*Fusarium cubense* E. F. Sm.) on condition that they are conveyed in packages containing not more than 10 plants, and that they are accompanied by a certificate indicating the number of plants and their origin. The certificate must be visaed by the French administrative or consular authority in the country of origin. After entry, the plants will be grown in quarantine for 1 year. (Order of March 28, 1928.)

Cocoa (*Theobroma cacao* L.): The importation, distribution, storage, and transit of plants, pods, and seeds of *Theobroma cacao*, as well as of soils and packing accompanying them, are prohibited both from countries declared infected by witches'-broom (*Marasmius perniciosus* Stahel) and from any country into which the importation of the said products is neither prohibited nor subjected to phytosanitary control.

The said products may be imported from countries not declared infected under an authorization obtained in advance which will determine in each case the number of plants admitted to importation on condition that they are conveyed in closed containers and are accompanied by a certificate of origin visaed by the French administrative or consular authority of the producing country, attesting that the plants have not been collected in a country in which the presence of the said disease has been determined, or in a country into which the importation of such plants is neither prohibited nor subjected to phytosanitary control. (Order of June 23, 1930.)

Coffee (*Coffea* spp.): The importation, distribution, storage, and transit of plants or parts thereof, fruits, and seeds, soils and packing accompanying them, are prohibited; provided, that beans for use as seed and in parchment may be imported from countries not declared infected by coffee rust (*Hemileia vastatrix* B. and Br.). These must be packed in perfectly closed metal receptacles weighing not more than 20 kg and accompanied by a certificate indicating the number of containers and the source of the seeds. The certificate must be visaed by the French administrative or consular authority of the country of origin and the seeds shall be disinfected on entry. For the importation of such beans from countries declared infected by the said disease, the importer shall obtain an import authorization in advance, and the beans shall be packed as above indicated and be accompanied by a certificate of origin issued by the phytosanitary service of the country of origin, attesting that the seeds were regularly disinfected before being placed in the containers. A second disinfection is required on entry.

Coffee plants may be imported under an authorization obtained in advance. They must be packed in closed sacks or other containers, free from debris of the coffee plant, and be accompanied by a phytosanitary certificate indicating origin and attesting that the plants are free from disease; the certificate must be visaed by the French consular authority. After inspection on arrival, the plants will either be destroyed or placed in quarantine for 1 year, according to the findings. (Order of March 28, 1928.)

Coffee (*Coffea* spp.) plants and parts thereof, dry or fresh coffee berries, coffee beans in parchment, hulled coffee seeds (fresh or unroasted), soil and composts, any sacks, cases, and packing that have served to transport those products, and all plants and parts thereof, and seeds capable of harboring the coffee berry borer (*Stephanoderes hampei*.Hagedorn), especially plants of *Rubus* and *Hibiscus:* Importation, distribution, storage, and transit prohibited of such products proceeding from Netherlands Indies, British West Indies, French Equatorial Africa, Belgian Congo, Brazil, and French West Africa, as well as from countries into which the importation of those products is not prohibited or subjected to phytosanitary control.

Authorization may be granted in the case of such products proceeding from other sources but only on presentation of a certificate issued by the competent authority of the country of origin, duly visaed, attesting that the said products had not been gathered in a region infested by the coffee berry borer, nor in a country into which the importation of those products is not prohibited or subjected to phytosanitary control. Entry permitted only through designated ports and on inspection showing the products to be free from parasites and apparently healthy. (General order of February 27, 1922.)

Cotton (*Gossypium* spp.): Importation, distribution, storage, and transit of plants, parts thereof, fruits, seed, cottonseed cake of any species of cotton, of *Hibiscus* or *Bauhinia*, and of soil or packing accompanying them, are prohibited to prevent the introduction of the pink bollworm (*Pectinophora gossypiella* Saund.); provided, that seeds may be imported, but only when delinted for use as seed, under the following conditions:

From countries not declared infested: They must be shipped in closed sacks or other receptacles, and be accompanied by a certificate of origin duly visaed. They will be disinfected on entry.

From a country declared infested: The importer must obtain an import authorization in advance. The seeds must be shipped in sacks or closed receptacles, sealed or marked by the phytosanitary service of the country of origin, and accompanied by a certificate of origin affirming that the seeds have been regularly disinfected. They will be disinfected again on entry.

Cotton lint for the local industries may be imported under the following conditions:

The importer must furnish advance notice of arrival to the phytosanitary inspector for each shipment. Bales of cotton will first be opened in the factory unless it is deemed necessary to make an examination in the port. Manufacturing wastes, especially the seeds and refuse thereof, will be burned and the packing disinfected by heat in the factory.

Plants of the family Malvaceae and of the genus *Bauhinia* within a radius of 300 m from the mill shall be destroyed. (Order of March 28, 1928.)

Fruits: Importation permitted of the following fruits originating in any country not declared infested by the Mediterranean fruitfly (*Ceratitis capitata* Wied.): *Achras sapota, Annona muricata, Artocarpus incisa, Averrhoa carambola, Carica papaya, C. quercifolia, Citrus bigarardia, C. indica, C. limonia, C. nobilis* and its hybrids, *C. aurantium, C. japonica, C. sinensis, C. decumana, Diospyros decandra, Eriobotrya japonica, Fortunella japonica, Garcinia mangostana, Litchi chinensis, Mangifera indica, Persea gratissima, Psidium guajava, Prunus armeniaca, P. persica* var. *nectarina, P. communis, Punica granatum, Pyrus communis,* and *P. malus,* subject to inspection by the phytosanitary service on arrival. If accompanied by a phytosanitary certificate, they will be exempt from any phytosanitary fee.

The importation of those fruits from the following countries known to be infested by the Mediterranean fruitfly (*Ceratitis capitata* Wied.) is prohibited: Azores, France, Greece, Italy, Madeira, Malta, Sicily, Spain, and Turkey in Europe.

Asia: Cyprus, Palestine, and Syria.

Africa: The African Continent, Canary Islands, Cape Verde Islands, and Mauritius.

America: Argentina, Bermuda, and Brazil.

Oceania: Australia, Hawaii, and New Zealand.

Exceptionally, the importation of those fruits is authorized from France, Algeria, Tunisia, Australia, and the Union of South Africa, which are declared to be infested by *Ceratitis capitata,* but which exercise on exported fruits a sanitary control offering sufficient guarantees. Fruit from these countries must be accompanied by a phytosanitary certificate of the country of origin; the fruits are also subject to inspection on arrival.

Hevea spp.: Importation, distribution, storage, and transit of plants and parts thereof, fruits, and seeds, as well as of soil and packing accompanying them, are prohibited; provided, that the seeds may be imported for planting only, when clean and free from hulls, and when they proceed exclusively from countries not declared infected by diseases and pests of that plant. Such seeds must be packed in closed sacks or receptacles and be accompanied by a duly visaed certificate indicating the number of packages and the source of the seeds. After inspection on arrival, the seeds will be delivered to the importer or disinfected.

Stocks or portions thereof may be imported exclusively from countries not declared infected, in closed receptacles and accompanied by a duly visaed certificate. After inspection on arrival, these stocks will either be destroyed or subjected to quarantine for 2 years. (Order of March 28, 1928.)

Sugarcane (*Saccharum officinarum* L.) : Importation, distribution, storage, and transit of plants, parts thereof, seeds, and of soils and packing accompanying them, are prohibited; provided, that the seeds may be imported exclusively for use as such. when free from hulls, under the following conditions:

From a country not declared infected.—They must be conveyed in perfectly closed metal receptacles and be accompanied by a duly visaed certificate indicating the name of the consignees and the source of the seeds. The seeds will be disinfected on entry.

From a country declared infected.—The importer shall obtain an import authorization in advance; the seeds shall be conveyed in perfectly closed metal receptacles marked by the phytosanitary service of the country of origin; the certificate shall attest that the seeds had been regularly disinfected before being packed. Such seeds shall again be disinfected on arrival.

Entire canes or parts thereof, stripped of leaves and roots, may be imported under an authorization obtained in advance, indicating the quantity of cuttings to be admitted and the special conditions, as well as under the following general conditions:

From a country not declared infected.—The canes shall be shipped in packages of not more than 50, in packing free from soil and cane refuse. They shall be accompanied by a duly visaed certificate indicating the number of packages and the origin of the cuttings. After a phytosanitary inspection, the cuttings will be destroyed or quarantined for 2 years.

From a country declared infected.—The canes must be shipped in packages of not more than 10, in containers sealed or marked by the phytosanitary service of the country of origin, attesting in the certificate of origin that each cutting was examined and found free from diseases. (Order of March 28, 1928, as amended by that of November 17, 1928.)

Tea (*Thea* spp.) : Importation, distribution, storage, and transit of plants, parts thereof, fruits, and seeds of all species of tea, and of soil and packing accompanying them, are prohibited; provided, that seeds exclusively for use as such may be introduced if accompanied by a certificate, issued by the phytosanitary service of the country of origin, indicating the number of packages, the source of the seeds, and attesting their freedom from diseases and parasites. After inspection at the port of entry, they will be delivered or disinfected. (Order of March 28, 1928.)

COUNTRIES DECLARED INFECTED

[Order of March 28, 1928]

The countries declared infected with respect to certain plants and plant products are as follows:

Sugarcane

Australia, Fiji, Taiwan (Formosa), Guinea, Hawaii, Japan, New Guinea, Philippines.

Hevea

The countries of South America.

Coffee

Belgian Congo, British West Indies, Equatorial Africa, Ivory Coast, Netherlands Indies, South America (countries of).

Cotton

Brazil, British East Africa, British India, British West Indies, Egypt, Hawaii, Madagascar, Mexico, Nigeria, Sierra Leone, United States (Louisiana, New Mexico, and Texas only).

Banana

The American Continent, Canary Islands, Gold Coast, Sierra Leone, West Indies.

AUTHORIZED PORT OF ENTRY

[Orders of July 1, 1927, and January 17, 1928]

The port of Saigon is opened for the importation of plants, soils, and materials for transportation covered by phytosanitary regulations.

MADAGASCAR AND DEPENDENCIES

(Including Ste-Marie-de-Madagascar, Nossi-Bé, Comoro Islands (Mayotte, Grand Comoro, Anjouan, and Moheli))

Banana plants (*Musa* spp.) : See order of December 7, 1926, page 25.
Cocoa (*Theobroma cacao* L.) : See order of December 3, 1929, page 26.
Coffee (*Coffea* spp.) : Plants and parts thereof, dry or fresh beans, coffee beans in parchment, hulled coffee beans (fresh or unroasted), soils or composts, packing and containers, and plants capable of harboring the coffee berry borer (*Stephanoderes hampei* Hag.) : See order of February 27, 1922, page 28.
Sugarcane (*Saccharum officinarum* L.) : See order of December 3, 1929, page 34.

MARTINIQUE

Banana plants (*Musa* spp.) : See orders of February 11, 1931, and February 9, 1935, applying the order of December 7, 1926, page 25.
Cocoa (*Theobroma cacao* L.) : See order of December 3, 1929, page 26.
Coffee (*Coffea* spp.) plants, berries, or seeds, and any product capable of distributing coffee rust (*Hemileia vastatrix* B. and Br.) : See order of May 19, 1924, page 30.
Coffee (*Coffea* spp.) plants and parts thereof, dry or fresh berries, beans in parchment, hulled beans (fresh or unroasted), soil and composts, packing and containers, and plants capable of harboring the coffee-berry borer (*Stephanoderes hampei* Hag.), especially *Hibiscus* and *Rubus:* See order of February 27, 1922, page 28.
Cotton (*Gossypium* spp.) : See order of February 22, 1926, page 32.
Sugarcane (*Saccharum officinarum* L.) : See order of December 3, 1929, page 34.

NEW CALEDONIA AND DEPENDENCIES

(Including Isle of Pines, Loyalty Islands, Huan Islands, Fortuna, and Alofi Islands, and the Wallis Islands)

Agricultural and horticultural products intended for consumption, as well as truck crops (culinary vegetables), seeds, and fruits for the same purpose: Importation unrestricted. See order of February 27, 1918, article 4, page 16.
Banana plants (*Musa* spp.) : See order of December 7, 1926, page 25.
Cocoa (*Theobroma cacao* L.) : See order of December 3, 1929, page 26.
Coconut (*Cocos nucifera* L.) : Importation of the nuts, hearts of coconut palms, and basket-making materials of coconut palm leaves from any source prohibited. See order of February 27, 1918, article 6, page 16.
Coffee (*Coffea* spp.) : Plants or parts thereof, dry or fresh berries, beans in parchment, hulled beans (fresh or unroasted), soil and composts, packing and containers, and plants capable of harboring the coffee-berry borer (*Stephanoderes hampei* Hag.), especially *Hibiscus* and *Rubus.* See order of February 27, 1922, page 28.

Potatoes (*Solanum tuberosum* L.) : Phytosanitary certificate issued by an authorized agent of the exporting country affirming freedom from all dangerous parasites. See order of February 27, 1918, article 7, page 17.

Sugarcane (*Saccharum officinarum* L.) : See order of December 3, 1929, page 34.

Trees, stocks, cuttings, leaves, roots, seeds, flower bulbs, soil and vegetable fertilizers, and other similar articles and their packing materials : See articles 1, 2, and 3 of the order of February 27, 1918, page 16.

GENERAL REGULATIONS ON THE IMPORTATION OF PLANTS, BULBS, AND SEEDS

[Order of February 27, 1918, as applied by Governor's decree No. 103 C of January 27, 1934]

ARTICLE 1. The introduction of trees, stocks, cuttings, leaves, roots, seeds, flower bulbs, soil and vegetable fertilizers, and other similar materials, as well as packing that has served for their transportation, is subject to the following restrictions :

Shipper's Declaration and Phytosanitary Certificate Required

ART. 2. The products mentioned in the preceding article must be accompanied by a shipper's declaration and a certificate issued by the competent authority of the place of origin, visaed by the French consular authority, if there is one, affirming that no special parasite or disease of the imported species exists in the country of origin.

Disinfection on Arrival Required

ART. 3. To be admitted into the Colony, the products, whatever their origin, shall be disinfected by a method to be determined by the local administration.

Any imported plant, seed, or product found on arrival to be infected or parasitized shall be destroyed at the expense of the importer.

Importation of Plant Products for Consumption Unrestricted

ART. 4. Agricultural and horticultural products intended for consumption, as well as truck crops (culinary vegetables), seeds, and fruits for the same use, are free from the preceding formalities.

ART. 5. Seeds for cooking are not restricted by any special measures.

Importation of Coconuts Prohibited

ART. 6. The importation into New Caledonia and Dependencies of coconuts, hearts of coconut palms, and basket-making materials of palm leaves from outside the archipelagoes of New Caledonia and Loyalty is rigorously prohibited. Any product in this category seized on arrival at Noumea will be destroyed by fire.

Potatoes Must Be Accompanied by a Certificate

ART. 7. Potatoes will not be admitted to importation unless they are accompanied by a phytosanitary certificate issued by an authorized agent of the exporting country, attesting that they have been examined and found free from all dangerous parasites.

Tubers found on arrival to be infested will be reladen or destroyed.

NEW HEBRIDES

(Including the Banks and Torres Islands)

Cocoa plants (*Theobroma cacao* L.) : See order of December 3, 1929, page 26.

Sugarcane (*Saccharum officinarum* L.) : See order of December 3, 1929, page 34.

OCEANIA, SETTLEMENTS IN

(Including Gambier Archipelago, Marquesas Islands, Tuamotou, French Leeward Islands, Society Islands, and Tubuai)

Banana plants (*Musa* spp.) : See the order of January 12, 1916, page 20, as rendered applicable to Oceania by that of February 11, 1931.

Cocoa plants (*Theobroma cacao* L.) : See the order of December 3, 1929, page 26.

Coconut (*Cocos nucifera* L.) palms and all plants and leaves of the palm family, and soils and composts that may carry their parasites: See order of January 12, 1916, as amended by that of November 15, 1924, page 20; also ministerial order of August 1, 1927, below.

Coffee (*Coffea* spp.) plants, berries, or seeds, and any product capable of distributing coffee rust (*Hemeleia vastatrix* B. and Br.) : See order of May 19, 1924, as rendered applicable to Oceania by the orders of January 12, 1916, and November 15, 1924, page 30.

Cotton (*Gossypium* spp.) plants or parts thereof, in the dry or green state, ginned or unginned cotton, cottonseed, soil or compost, and packing or containers thereof: See order of February 22, 1926, page 32.

Sugarcane (*Saccharum officinarum* L.) : See order of December 3, 1929, page 34.

IMPORTATION OF COCONUT PALMS, NUTS, AND LEAVES PROHIBITED

[Ministerial Order of August 1, 1927]

ARTICLE 1. The importation by sea, the distribution, storage, and transit of coconut palms, coconuts, and leaves of the coconut palm, and of any other material that may contain parasites which attack this palm are prohibited for the French Settlement of India and Oceania.

OCEANIA

GENERAL REGULATIONS

[Order of January 12, 1916, as amended by that of November 15, 1924, also the order of August 1, 1927]

Entry of Coconut Palms, Coffee, and Banana Plants Prohibited

ARTICLE 1. The entry by sea into the Settlements of Oceania is prohibited of coconut trees (*Cocos nucifera* L.) and all other plants of the palm family, coffee (*Coffea* spp.), banana and other Musaceae and their fruits, leaves, or branches, and soils or composts that may carry parasites of those plants.

Certification of Merchandise from Tropical Regions

ART. 2. Merchandise proceeding from tropical regions may be unladen only on a certificate issued by the customs service, affirming that the packing does not consist of hay, straw, fiber, or any other agricultural product that may represent a danger from the agricultural point of view. In case of doubt or dispute, recourse shall be made to the chief pharmacist in the Service of the Colonial Hospital and/or the crop agent (agent de culture) in charge of the Station of Agriculture and Animal Husbandry.

Phytosanitary Certificate Required for Other Plants

ART. 3. No living plants or parts thereof, stocks, cuttings, buds, other than those mentioned in article 1, including seeds, shall be admitted into the Colony unless they are accompanied by a certificate indicating the name and address of the shipper and the place of origin of the products; that document, duly countersigned by an inspector or an agent of the phytosanitary service of the country of origin, shall affirm that the plants or seeds are not infested by any disease; that they do not proceed from a contaminated locality, or that they have been disinfected and, especially with respect to coffee seeds, that *Hemileia* does not exist in the country of origin. Furthermore, unlading may be effected only after the said certificate, visaed by the customs service, shall have been signed by the chief pharmacist or the crop agent.

REUNION ISLAND

Banana plants (*Musa* spp.) : See order of December 7, 1926, page 25.

Cocoa plants (*Theobroma cacao* L.) : See order of December 3, 1929, page 26.

Coffee (*Coffea* spp.) plants and parts thereof, dry or fresh beans, beans in parchment, hulled beans (fresh or unroasted), soil and composts, packing and containers, and plants capable of harboring the coffee-berry borer (*Stephanoderes hampei* Hag.) : See order of February 27, 1922, page 28.

Cotton (*Gossypium* spp.) plants or parts thereof in the dry or green state, ginned or unginned cotton, cottonseed, soil or compost, packing or containers that have served to transport those products, and any plants, seeds or parts thereof capable of harboring the pink bollworm, especially *Hibiscus cannabinus*, *H. esculentus*, and *Bauhinia:* See order of February 22, 1926, page 32.

Sugarcane (*Saccharum officinarum* L.) : See order of December 3, 1929, page 34.

SOMALILAND

Cotton (*Gossypium* spp.) plants or parts thereof in the dry or green state, ginned or unginned cotton, cottonseed, soil or compost, packing or containers that have served to transport those products, and any seeds, plants, or parts thereof capable of harboring the pink bollworm, especially *Hibiscus cannabinus*, *H. esculentus*, and *Bauhinia:* See order of February 22, 1926, page 32.

Sugarcane (*Saccharum officinarum* L.) : See order of December 3, 1929, page 34.

TOGOLAND

Banana plants (*Musa* spp.) : See order of December 7, 1926, page 25, as applied to Togoland by the order of February 11, 1931.

Cocoa plants (*Theobroma cacao* L.) : See order of December 3, 1929, as applied to Togoland by the order of February 13, 1932, page 26.

Coffee (*Coffea* spp.) plants, berries, seeds, or any product capable of distributing coffee rust (*Hemileia vastatrix* B. and Br.) : See order of May 19, 1924, page 30, as applied to Togoland by the order of July 30, 1924.

Cotton (*Gossypium* spp.) plants or parts thereof in the dry or green state, ginned or unginned cotton, cottonseed, soil or compost, packing or containers that have served to transport those articles, and any seeds, plants, or parts thereof capable of harboring the pink bollworm, especially of *Hibiscus cannabinus*, *H. esculentus*, and *Bauhinia:* See order of February 22, 1926, page 32.

Sugarcane (*Saccharum officinarum* L.) : See order of December 3, 1929, page 34.

WEST AFRICA

(Including Dahomey, Guinea, Ivory Coast, Mauritania, Niger, Senegal, and Sudan)

Banana plants (*Musa* spp.) : To prevent the introduction of Panama wilt disease (*Fusarium cubense* E. F. Sm.), banana plants may be imported into French West Africa only through the ports of Dakar, Conakry, Port Bouët, Sassandra, and Cotonou, to the exclusion of all points on the land frontiers. (Order of June 13, 1935, modifying that of March 14, 1927, under the provisions of the order of December 7, 1926, which see, p. 25.)

Cocoa plants (*Theobroma cacao* L.) : See order of December 3, 1929, page 26.

Coffee (*Coffea* spp.) plants, berries, or seeds, and any product capable of distributing coffee rust (*Hemileia vastatrix* B. and Br.): See order of May 19, 1924, page 30.

Cotton (*Gossypium* spp.) plants or parts thereof in the dry or green state, ginned or unginned cotton, cottonseed, soil or compost, packing or containers that have served to transport these products, and any seeds, plants, or parts thereof capable of harboring the pink bollworm, especially plants of *Hibiscus cannabinus, H. esculentus,* and *Bauhinia:* See order of February 22, 1926, page 32.

Sugarcane (*Saccharum officinarum* L.): See order of December 3, 1929, page 34.

GENERAL QUARANTINES APPLYING TO DESIGNATED COLONIES

BANANA PLANTS (*Musa* spp.)

[Order of December 7, 1926, as amended by that of February 9, 1935]

IMPORTATION PROHIBITED FROM COUNTRIES INFECTED BY PANAMA DISEASE

ARTICLE 1. The importation into, distribution and storage in, and transit through the French colonies named in article 6 of the present order, are prohibited of banana plants proceeding from countries in which the presence of the Panama wilt disease (*Fusarium cubense* E. F. Sm.) has been determined, or from those into which the importation of the said plants is neither prohibited nor subjected to phytosanitary control.

ENTRY FROM OTHER SOURCES PERMITTED UNDER CERTIFICATION

ART. 2. The movements of banana plants from any source indicated in article 1 in the French colonies named in article 6 may be authorized only on presentation of a certificate issued by the competent authority of the country of origin, attesting that the said plants were neither collected in a region where the Panama wilt disease had been determined nor in a country into which the importation of the said plants is neither prohibited nor subjected to phytosanitary control.

IRREGULAR SHIPMENTS DENIED ENTRY

ART. 3. Any of the above-mentioned plants offered for importation into the French colonies named in article 6 not meeting the provisions of articles 1 and 2 will be reladen immediately or seized and destroyed by fire at the expense of the holder.

This applies also to shipments for which the importer does not furnish a valid certificate of origin.

ENTRY PERMITTED AT DESIGNATED PORTS ONLY

ART. 4. For plants offered for entry under one of the forms indicated in article 1 and accompanied by the certificate prescribed by article 2, the authorization for importation, distribution, storage, or transit in the French colonies named in article 6 may be granted only in one of the points of entry designated for each colony by an order of the local administration, granted only after an inspection by the authority designated by the Governor, showing the products to be apparently healthy and free from the parasite referred to in the present order.

SUSPECTED LOTS DENIED ENTRY

ART. 4 contd. Any suspected lot will be reladen immediately or seized and destroyed by fire at the expense of the holder.

IMPORTATIONS FROM INFECTED COUNTRIES EXCEPTIONALLY PERMITTED

ART. 5. Provides for derogations from the preceding provisions from prescribed sources, for material of a real technical or economic interest, through administrative channels.

COLONIES CONCERNED

ART. 6. The provisions of this order are applicable to banana plants for importation into and transit through the following French colonies: Cameroons, Equatorial Africa, Guadeloupe, Guiana, Indo-China, Madagascar, Martinique, New Caledonia, Oceania (Settlements of), Togoland, and West Africa.

INFECTED COUNTRIES

The provisions of article 1 are applicable to the designated products proceeding from the American Continent, Canary Islands, French Guiana, Gold Coast, Guadeloupe, Martinique, and Sierra Leone.

COCOA PLANTS (*Theobroma cacao* L.)

[Order of December 3, 1929, as amended by that of February 13, 1932]

IMPORTATION FROM CERTAIN COUNTRIES PROHIBITED ON ACCOUNT OF WITCHES'-BROOM

ARTICLE 1. The importation into, distribution and storage in, and transit through the French colonies named in article 7 of cacao plants (*Theobroma cacao* L.) proceeding from a country in which the presence of witches'-broom (*Marasmius perniciosus* Stahel) has been determined or from any country into which the importation of the said plants is neither prohibited nor subjected to phytosanitary control, are prohibited.

IMPORTATION FROM OTHER SOURCES RESTRICTED

ART. 2. The importation, distribution, storage, and transit in the French colonies named in article 7, paragraph 1, of cacao plants from any source other than those named in article 7, paragraph 2, may be authorized, but only on presentation of a certificate issued by competent authority of the country of origin that the said plants have neither been collected in a region in which the disease called "witches'-broom" has been determined, nor in a country into which the importation of the said plants has not been prohibited or subjected to phytosanitary control. The certificate is not valid unless visaed by the consuls, vice-consuls, or consular agents of the French Republic in foreign countries.

IRREGULAR SHIPMENTS DENIED ENTRY

ART. 3. Any cacao plants offered for importation into the French colonies named in article 7 of the present order that do not meet the provisions of articles 1 and 2 will be reladen immediately or seized and destroyed by fire at the expense of the holder.

The same applies if the importer fails to furnish a valid certificate.

IMPORTATION PERMITTED THROUGH DESIGNATED PORTS ONLY

ART. 4. Authorization for the importation, distribution, storage, and transit in the French colonies named in article 7 can be granted only for cacao plants accompanied by the certificate prescribed in article 2 of the present order and through a customs office designated by an order of the local administration; the authorization will not be definitely granted until an inspection by the designated authority shows the products to be apparently healthy and free from the parasite mentioned.

Any suspected lot will be reladen immediately at the expense of the holder, or seized and destroyed by fire.

IMPORTATION FROM CONTAMINATED COUNTRIES EXCEPTIONALLY PERMITTED

ART. 5. For the introduction into French colonies of cacao plants originating in one of the contaminated countries named in article 7 or in a region into which the importation of the said plants is not prohibited or subjected to phytosanitary control, derogations may be exceptionally granted by decision of the Minister of Colonies establishing therein the conditions under which the importation may be effected and indicating the quantities and varieties of plants whose importation is authorized.

Such derogations may be granted only for plants whose introduction is believed to present a real economic and technical interest, and may be imported through diplomatic channels alone, and when accompanied by a phytosanitary certificate attesting the freedom of the plants from disease.

ART. 6. The same provisions are applicable to fresh cacao pods and seeds.

FRENCH COLONIES CONCERNED

ART. 7. The provisions of the present order are applicable to plants, pods, and seeds of *Theobroma cacao* offered for importation into and transit through Equatorial Africa, Guadeloupe, Guiana, Madagascar, Martinique, New Caledonia, New Hebrides, Oceania (Settlements of), Reunion, and West Africa.

COUNTRIES AFFECTED

The prohibitions of article 1 are applicable to the designated products proceeding from South America, Central America, and Trinidad.

RESTRICTIONS ON THE IMPORTATION OF COFFEE

[Order of February 27, 1922, as amended]

IMPORTATION PROHIBITED ON ACCOUNT OF THE COFFEE BERRY BORER

ARTICLE 1. Importation into, movement and storage in, and transit through French colonies that are free from the coffee berry borer (*Stephanoderes hampei* Hagedorn) are prohibited of any products capable of distributing that insect, and such products proceeding either from countries in which the presence of that pest has been demonstrated or from those into which the importation of those products is not prohibited or subjected to a phytosanitary control.

PRODUCTS AFFECTED

This prohibition applies to coffee plants and parts thereof, to dry or fresh coffee berries, to coffee beans in parchment, hulled coffee beans (fresh or unroasted), soil and composts, and to sacks, cases, and packing that have served to transport the aforesaid products, as well as to all plants or parts thereof and seeds capable of harboring the coffee berry borer, especially *Hibiscus* and *Rubus*.

IMPORTATION UNDER CERTIFICATION

ART. 2. The movements indicated in article 1 of the said products proceeding from sources other than those indicated in that article may be authorized only on the presentation of a certificate, issued by the competent authority of the country of origin, attesting that the said products had not been gathered in a region where the presence of *Stephanoderes* had been determined, nor in a country into which the importation of the said products is not prohibited or subjected to phytosanitary control. The certificate must be visaed by the consular or other authorized official of the French Republic.

IMPORTATION INTO NONPRODUCING COLONIES

ART. 2 contd. In colonies that do not produce coffee, a derogation of the presentation of the certificate required by paragraph 1 of this article may be granted by Ministerial decision for coffees proceeding direct from warehouses of the metropolis (European France) or from countries declared contaminated, on condition that they are intended for consumption only.

In all other colonies, that derogation may be granted only when it is shown on entry into their territory that a technical inspection of imported plant products has been established and completed by the necessary equipment for quarantine and disinfection.

DISPOSAL OF IRREGULAR SHIPMENTS

ART. 3. Such products, offered for importation into the French colonies named in article 5, as do not meet the provisions of articles 1 and 2 will be reladen immediately or seized and destroyed by fire at the expense of the holder.

The same applies to those for which the importer does not furnish a certificate of origin recognized as valid.

ENTRY LIMITED TO DESIGNATED PORTS

ART. 4. Prescribes that the said products may enter only through the ports designated for each colony and subject to inspection on arrival.

Any suspected lot will be reladen immediately or seized and destroyed by fire at the expense of the holder.

COLONIES CONCERNED

ART. 5. The provisions of this order are applicable to the products named in article 1 and offered for importation into or transit through Guadeloupe, Guiana, Indo-China, Madagascar, Martinique, New Caledonia, and Reunion.

COUNTRIES OF ORIGIN CONCERNED

ART. 5 contd. The above prohibitions are applicable to the designated products proceeding from Belgian Congo, Brazil, British West Indies, French Equatorial Africa, French West Africa, and Netherlands Indies, as well as from countries into which the importation of the said products is neither prohibited nor subjected to phytosanitary control.

RESTRICTIONS ON THE IMPORTATION OF COFFEE

[Order of May 19, 1924]

IMPORTATION FROM CERTAIN COUNTRIES PROHIBITED ON ACCOUNT OF COFFEE RUST

ARTICLE 1. The importation into, distribution and storage in, and transit through the French colonies named in article 6 that are free from coffee rust (*Hemileia vastatrix* B. and Br.) of any product capable of distributing that disease, proceeding from any country in which the presence of *Hemileia vastatrix* has been determined, or from those into which the importation of the said products is not prohibited or subjected to phytosanitary control, are prohibited.

ENTRY FROM OTHER SOURCES UNDER CERTIFICATION

ART. 2. The importation, distribution, storage, and transit in the French colonies named in article 6 of the products referred to in article 1, proceeding from sources other than those mentioned in that article, may be authorized on presentation of a certificate issued by competent authority of the country of origin. The certificate shall affirm that the said products were not collected in a locality in which *Hemileia vastatrix* has been determined, nor in a country into which the importation of the said products is not prohibited or subjected to phytosanitary control. The certificate must be visaed by a French consul, vice consul, or consular agent in foreign countries.

IRREGULAR SHIPMENTS DENIED ENTRY

ART. 3. Any of the above-mentioned products presented for importation into the French colonies named in article 6 that do not meet the provisions of articles 1 and 2 will be reladen immediately or seized and destroyed by fire at the expense of the holder. The same applies to shipments for which the importer fails to furnish a valid certificate as prescribed in article 2.

ENTRY OF COFFEE SEEDS EXCEPTIONALLY PERMITTED FROM INFECTED COUNTRIES

ART. 4. Coffee seeds intended for sowing proceeding either from a country declared contaminated by *Hemileia vastatrix* or from one into which the products mentioned in article 1 are neither prohibited nor subjected to phytosanitary control may, exceptionally, be introduced into the French colonies named in article 6 under a special authorization of the Governor General or Governor after disinfection.

ENTRY LIMITED TO DESIGNATED PORTS

ART. 5. Prescribes that the products concerned shall enter the designated French colonies only through ports authorized by the respective local administrations, subject to inspection on arrival.

COLONIES CONCERNED

ART. 6. The provisions of this order are applicable to the following French colonies which are declared free from *Hemileia vastatrix:* Equatorial Africa, Guadeloupe, Guiana, Martinique, Oceania, Togoland, and West Africa.

INFECTED COUNTRIES

ART. 6 contd. The prohibitions prescribed in article 1 of the present order are applicable to the designated products proceeding from any country of Africa, Asia, and Oceania, as well as from any country into which the importation of the said products is neither prohibited nor subjected to phytosanitary control.

COTTON IMPORT RESTRICTION

[Order of February 22, 1926, as amended]

IMPORTATION OF COTTON AND COTTONSEED PROHIBITED FROM COUNTRIES INFESTED BY THE PINK BOLLWORM

ARTICLE 1. The importation into, movement or storage in, and transit through French colonies that are free from pink bollworm ((*Gelechia*) *Pectinophora gossypiella* Saund.) of all products capable of distributing that insect, proceeding either from countries in which the presence of the pink bollworm has been determined, or from countries that do not prohibit the importation of the said products or subject them to phytosanitary control, are prohibited.

PRODUCTS AFFECTED

This prohibition applies to entire cotton plants or parts thereof in the green or the dry state, ginned or unginned cotton, cottonseed, soil, composts, sacks, cases, or packing that have served to transport the articles just mentioned, as well as to any seeds, entire plants or parts thereof, capable of harboring the pink bollworm, especially *Hibiscus cannabinus, H. esculentus,* and *Bauhinia.*

IMPORTATION FROM OTHER SOURCES RESTRICTED—CERTIFICATE REQUIRED

ART. 2. The importation into, movement or storage in, and transit through the French colonies named in article 6 of the products referred to in article 1, of other origins than those indicated in that article, may be authorized only on presentation of a certificate issued by the competent authority of the country of origin attesting that the said products were not gathered in a region where the presence of the pink bollworm had been determined, or in any country into which the importation of the said products is not prohibited or subjected to a phytosanitary control.

The certificate will not be valid unless it bears the visa of the Governor General, the Governor, the resident superior, or their delegates, in matters pertaining to the French colonies; of the Governor General, residence general, or their delegates in Algeria, Tunisia, and Morocco, and that of the consuls, vice consuls, or consular agents of the French Republic in foreign countries.

IRREGULAR SHIPMENTS RELADEN OR DESTROYED

ART. 3. Any of the above products offered for importation into the French colonies named in article 6 that do not meet the conditions prescribed in articles 1 and 2 above, will be reladen immediately or seized and destroyed by fire at the expense of the holder.

The same applies to the said products for which the importer does not furnish a certificate of origin recognized as valid.

ART. 4. Prescribes that the said products shall enter the respective French colonies only through designated ports and subject to inspection on arrival at those ports.

Suspected shipments will be reladen at once, or seized and destroyed by fire at the expense of the holder.

SMALL LOTS OF COTTONSEED EXCEPTED SUBJECT TO DISINFECTION

ART. 5. For the introduction into the French colonies of very small lots of cottonseed originating in any of the contaminated countries named in article 6 or in a region into which the importation of cottonseed is not prohibited or subjected to phytosanitary control, derogations may be granted, exceptionally, by decision of the Minister of Colonies, indicating the quantities and varieties of seeds for which the importation is authorized. Such derogations may be granted only for seeds whose introduction is deemed to present a real technical or economic interest and after a disinfection made and guaranteed by the service qualified for that purpose, either in France or on arrival in the colony. Each such shipment must be accompanied by a disinfection certificate expressly mentioning the ministerial decision, the quantity of seeds disinfected, and the method of disinfection employed.

COLONIES CONCERNED

ART. 6. The provisions of the present order are applicable to the products named in article 1 offered for importation into or transit through all French colonies except Equatorial Africa, Guadeloupe, Indo-China (Cambodia and Cochin China only), Madagascar, New Caledonia, and New Hebrides. In other words, they are applicable to: Cameroons, Guiana, India (Settlements in), Martinique, Oceania (Settlements in), Reunion, Somaliland, Togoland, and West Africa.

COUNTRIES TO WHICH THE PROHIBITION IS APPLICABLE

ART. 6 contd. The prohibitions of article 1 are applicable to the designated products proceeding from Anglo-Egyptian Sudan, Angola, Asia (except Indo-China, Tonkin, and Annam), Australia, Belgian Congo, Brazil, British East Africa, British West Indies, Egypt, French Equatorial Africa, German East Africa (old colonies of), Greece, Guadeloupe, Hawaii, Italian Somaliland, Lagos, Madagascar, Mexico, Morocco, New Caledonia, New Hebrides, Nigeria, Samoa, Sierra Leone, Tunisia, United States (Louisiana, New Mexico, and Texas only), and Zanzibar.

SUGARCANE (SACCHARUM OFFICINARUM L.)

[Order of December 3, 1929]

IMPORTATION PROHIBITED FROM ALL FRENCH COLONIES EXCEPT INDO-CHINA

ARTICLE 1. The importation into, distribution and storage in, and transit through the French colonies of plants, cuttings, or seeds of sugarcane from whatever source, are prohibited. This does not apply to Indo-China.

ENTRY OF SMALL LOTS EXCEPTIONALLY PERMITTED

ART. 2. For the introduction into the French colonies of a small number of plants or cuttings stripped of their leaves and leaf sheaths, as well as seeds of sugarcane, originating in any country whatever, derogation may exceptionally be granted, by decision of the Minister of Colonies, establishing the conditions under which importation may be effected and indicating the quantities and varieties of plants, cuttings, and seeds of which importation is authorized.

Derogations may be granted only for plants or cuttings whose introduction is deemed of real economic or technical interest. Such plants may be shipped through administrative channels only and at the importer's expense. Entry may be made only through customs offices designated by each colony and only when inspection on arrival shows that the products are apparently healthy and free from any parasite.

Each suspected lot will be at once reladen or seized and destroyed by fire at the expense of the holder.

ADMITTED SUGARCANE KEPT UNDER OBSERVATION

Any lot of sugarcane that is admitted will be taken in charge by the local agricultural service, which will grow the plants and keep them under observation for the necessary time, namely, a minimal period of 3 months. Plants then found healthy will be delivered; any plant found to be diseased will be destroyed by fire without indemnity to the importers.

B. E. P. Q. 466.

PLANT-QUARANTINE IMPORT RESTRICTIONS, BRITISH COLONY OF FIJI

OCTOBER 21, 1937.

This summary of the plant-quarantine import restrictions of the British Colony of Fiji has been prepared for the information of nurserymen, plant-quarantine officials, and others interested in the exportation of plants and plant products to that Colony.

It was prepared by Harry B. Shaw, plant quarantine inspector, in charge of Foreign Information Service, Division of Foreign Plant Quarantines, from the Noxious Weeds and Diseases of Plants Ordinance, No. 21, of November 18, 1929, and proclamations made thereunder, and reviewed by the Director of Agriculture of the Colony of Fiji.

The information contained in this circular is believed to be correct and complete up to the time of preparation, but it is not intended to be used independently of, nor as a substitute for, the original texts, and it is not to be interpreted as legally authoritative.

LEE A. STRONG,
Chief, Bureau of Entomology and Plant Quarantine.

PLANT-QUARANTINE IMPORT RESTRICTIONS, BRITISH COLONY OF FIJI

BASIC LEGISLATION

[Noxious Weeds and Diseases of Plants ordinance No. 21, November 18, 1929]

This ordinance empowers the Governor in Council to prohibit the importation into the Colony of any plant, including plants generally, or, specified plants from any designated place, and either absolutely or conditionally.

AUTHORIZED PORTS OF ENTRY

Section 5 of the ordinance prescribes that no plants shall be imported into the Colony except through the ports of Suva, Levuka, or Lautoka, or such other ports as may be authorized by the Governor.

PHYTOSANITARY CERTIFICATE REQUIRED

The same section prescribes that every importation of plants whether for sale or for private use must be accompanied by a certificate signed by an officer of the Department of Agriculture, or other department to which the duties relating to horticulture are assigned, of the country or place where the plants were grown or whence they were imported, certifying that the plants are free from disease.

ADMINISTRATIVE REGULATIONS

[Noxious Weeds and Diseases of Plants Regulations, November 12, 1930]

DEFINITIONS

ARTICLE 1. In these Regulations —
"Plant" means any tree, flower, shrub, vegetable, or other vegetable growth; and includes the expression "part of plant", which in turn includes any root,

corm, tuber, bulb, stem, leaf, cutting, bud, graft, seed, fruit, or any portion thereof.

"Fruit" means any edible product of any plant and includes the peel, skin, or shell of fruit.

"Diseases of plants" means any insect, pest, or disease in any form or stage of development which is or may be injurious to plants.

INSPECTION AND TREATMENT OF IMPORTED PLANTS

ART. 2. *Landing of plants.*—No officer of customs shall permit plants to be landed from a vessel except on the written instruction of an inspector.

ART. 3. *Imported plants subject to inspection.*—All plants, and the packages and the wrappings that contain or have contained the same, imported into the Colony shall be liable to detention and examination by an inspector and shall be subject to the following treatment:

(*a*) Plants affected by any species of fruitfly or borer shall be destroyed forthwith.

(*b*) Plants affected by any insect pest, other than fruitfly or borer, shall be fumigated under the directions of an inspector.

ART. 4. *Restrictions on entry of soil.*—No soil shall be imported into the Colony except with the written permission first obtained of the Director of Agriculture. Provided that all soil so imported shall be fumigated with carbon disulphide under the direction and to the satisfaction of an inspector.

ART. 5. (1) *Inspector's certificate necessary for release of plants.*—After the inspection and treatment, if any, of plants brought into the Colony, an inspector shall issue a certificate setting forth that the plants have been inspected and fumigated or otherwise treated and showing the sums payable in respect of the fumigation or other treatment, if such has been given.

(2) Upon presentation to the proper officer of customs of an inspector's certificate, together with an acknowledgment of the payment of fees, if any, due in respect of treatment of plants, an importer may with such officer's consent remove from the fumigating station the articles to which the certificate relates.

ART. 6. *Plants not included in certificate liable to seizure and destruction.*— All imported plants and the packages or wrappings that contain or have contained them may be seized and destroyed by direction of an inspector if, on demand made by an inspector or customs officer, sufficient evidence of their being included in the certificate issued in the country of origin or export is not given by their importer.

SPECIAL REGULATIONS

[Proclamation No. 4, January 18, 1933]

Import permit required.—The importation of all plants into the Colony is prohibited unless a written permit for their importation is first obtained from the Director of Agriculture in which permit the conditions of such importation may be specified. Provided that the following plants may be imported without permits.

EXCEPTIONS

. .(*a*) .All plants imported from Great Britain, Australia, Canada, New Zealand, and the United States of America, except those specified in schedule 1, provided that permits shall be required in respect of the fruits of the plants set out in schedule 2 imported from Australia and in respect of growing plants of the natural order Rosaceae imported from Canada, New Zealand, and the United States.

(*b*) Copra from the Kingdom of Tonga.

Certification of forage crop seeds and plants required.—Importations of seeds, live stems, and whole plants of pasture and fodder grasses and clovers shall be accompanied by certificates in the form set out in schedule 3, signed by a responsible officer of the Department of Agriculture of the country in which they were grown, certifying that the district in which they were produced is entirely free from cattle tick infestation.

Unrestricted plant products.—The provisions of this proclamation shall not apply to fibers in an unmanufactured condition or to any parts of plants which have undergone any process of manufacture, except copra, provided that they are not in a damp or decomposed condition.

Plant material may be seized and destroyed or disinfected.—The Director of Agriculture, at his discretion, may decline to issue a permit, and he or an inspector acting directly under his instructions shall have the power to prevent the landing of, or to seize and destroy without paying compensation for such destruction, any plant matter imported from any country whether a permit for the importation of such plant matter has been issued or not, to retain such plant matter for fumigation or for observation for any period of time, or to require any plant matter imported to be planted in such area as he shall direct and under such quarantine measures as he may deem to be advisable, and any such plant matter shall not be removed from such areas without the written authority of the Director of Agriculture.

SCHEDULE 1

Cabbages.	Grass seed.
Cauliflowers.	Lettuce.
Citrus plants.	Pineapples.
Clover seed.	Seed cotton.
Coconuts.	Sugarcane.
Cottonseed.	Tobacco seed.
Cut flowers.	Unhusked rice (paddy).

Live stems and whole plants of pasture and fodder grasses, chaff, hay, and straw, whether or not used for packing.

SCHEDULE 2

Amygdalus (Prunus) persica L., peach.
Carica papaya L., papaya or pawpaw.
Citrus aurantium L., Seville orange, and varieties.
Citrus nobilis deliciosa Swingle, Mandarin type of orange.
Coffea arabica L., coffee.
Eugenia braziliensis Lam., Brazil cherry.
Eugenia jambos L., rose apple, Malabar plum.
Eugenia malaccensis L., mountain or Malayapple or large-fruited rose apple.
Mangifera indica L., mango.
Opuntia tuna Mill., pricklypear.
Opuntia vulgaris Mill., barberry fig.
Passiflora quadrangularis L., giant granadilla.
Persea (gratissima) americana Mill., avocado.
Prunus armeniaca L., apricot.
Prunus cerasus L., cherry, all varieties.
Psidium cattleianum S., strawberry guava.
Psidium guajava L., guava and varieties.

SCHEDULE 3 [4]

I hereby certify that the shipment of grass plants and seeds marked _____, No. of packages _____, contents _____, addressed to _____, sent by _____, per _____, was produced in a district free from cattle tick infection.

> Signature of officer_____
> Official title_____
> Address _____ ____ _____
> Date_____

PENALTIES IMPOSED FOR VIOLATIONS OF THE PLANT QUARANTINE ACT

According to reports received by the Bureau during the period October 1 to December 31, 1937, penalties have recently been imposed by the proper Federal authorities for violations of the Plant Quarantine Act, as follows:

JAPANESE BEETLE QUARANTINE

In the case of the *United States* v. *Raymond Peacock*, Rochester, N. Y., in the interstate transportation of a truckload of cantaloups from a point in the regu-

---

[4] This certificate can be furnished by the Bureau of Animal Industry only.

lated area to a point outside thereof, without inspection and certification, the defendant pleaded guilty and was fined $25.

In the case of the *United States* v. *Max Goldblatt*, Rochester, N. Y., in the interstate transportation of a truckload of cantaloups from a point in the regulated area to a point outside thereof, without inspection and certification, the defendant pleaded guilty and was fined $25.

In the case of the *United States* v. *Nat Barnett*, Rochester, N. Y., in the interstate transportation of a truckload of tomatoes and peppers from a point in the regulated area to a point outside thereof, without inspection and certification, the defendant pleaded guilty and was fined $25.

In the case of the *United States* v. *John Pitts*, Walworth, N. Y., in the interstate transportation of a truckload of peppers from a point in the regulated area to a point outside thereof, without inspection and certification, the defendant pleaded guilty and was fined $25.

In the case of the *United States* v. *Phillip Fostano*, Rochester, N. Y., in the interstate transportation of a truckload of watermelons from a point in the regulated area to a point outside thereof, without inspection and certification, the defendant pleaded guilty and was fined $25.

In the case of the *United States* v. *Max Pies*, Rochester, N. Y., in the interstate transportation of a truckload of cantaloups from a point in the regulated area to a point outside thereof, without inspection and certification, the defendant pleaded guilty and was fined $25.

In the case of the *United States* v. *Mike Mastrolenardo*, Rochester, N. Y., in the interstate transportation of a truckload each of peppers and eggplants from a point in the regulated area to a point outside thereof, without inspection and certification, the defendant pleaded guilty and was fined $25.

In the case of the *United States* v. *John Chichelli*, Rochester, N. Y., in the interstate transportation of two truckloads of peppers, tomatoes, watermelons, and cantaloups from a point in the regulated area to a point outside thereof, without inspection and certification, the defendant pleaded guilty and was fined $25.

In the case of the *United States* v. *Sebastian Scacciafero*, Rochester, N. Y., in the interstate transportation of a truckload of cantaloups from a point in the regulated area to a point outside thereof, without inspection and certification, the defendant pleaded guilty and was fined $25.

In the case of the *United States* v. *Patsy Columbo*, Rochester, N. Y., in the interstate transportation of a truckload of peppers from a point in the regulated area to a point outside thereof, without inspection and certification, the defendant pleaded guilty and was fined $25.

In the case of the *United States* v. *Harry Rosenstein*, Buffalo, N. Y., in the interstate transportation of cantaloups from a point in the regulated area to a point outside thereof, without inspection and certification, the defendant pleaded guilty and was fined $25.

In the case of the *United States* v. *Lawrence Shapiro*, Vineland, N. J., in the interstate transportation of a truckload of potatoes from a point in the regulated area to a point outside thereof, without inspection and certification, the defendant pleaded guilty and was fined $25. (P. Q. case 495.)

In the case of the *United States* v. *Harry Richards*, Pedricktown, N. J., in the interstate transportation of a truckload of peppers and eggplants from a point in the regulated area to a point outside thereof, without inspection and certification, the defendant pleaded guilty and was fined $25. (P. Q. case 498.)

In the case of the *United States* v. *Paul R. Turner*, Bridgeton, N. J., in the interstate transportation of a truckload of peppers, eggplants, and tomatoes from a point in the regulated area to a point outside thereof, without inspection and certification, the defendant pleaded guilty and was fined $25. (P. Q. case 499.)

In the case of the *United States* v. *William H. Harris*, Newfield, N. J., in the interstate transportation of a truckload of apples, eggplants, and tomatoes from a point in the regulated area to a point outside thereof, without inspection and certification, the defendant pleaded guilty and was fined $25. (P. Q. case 500.)

In the case of the *United States* v. *Vaughan's Seed Store, Inc.*, New York, N. Y., for the misuse of Japanese beetle certificates in connection with two shipments of ivy to Florida, the defendant pleaded guilty and was fined $50 on each count. The fine was remitted.

QUARANTINES AFFECTING MEXICAN PRODUCTS

In the case of the United States versus the persons listed below, for attempting to smuggle in contraband plant material, the penalties indicated were imposed by the United States customs officials at the following ports:

Name	Port	Contraband	Penalty
Fernando Martinez	Calexico, Calif	9 pieces sugarcane	$1.00
R. E. Smith	Brownsville, Tex	6 guavas	1.00
Mrs. Julia Alvarado	do	1 apple	1.00
Candalaria Lopez	do	5 oranges	1.00
Patricio Villareal	do	5 oranges and 1 apple	1.00
Guadeleupe Arce de Guajardo	Eagle Pass, Tex	12 quinces and 11 sweet limes	1.00
Manuel Colloza	do	1 orange	1.00
Rosa Vasquez Arrendo	do	8 avocados	1.00
Antonio G. Rodriquez	Hidalgo, Tex	1 avocado	1.00
Margarita Tijerina	do	do	1.00
Monica de Anda	do	1 apple	1.00
Julio Guerra	do	20 avocados	2.00
Angela T. DeVirreal	Laredo, Tex	1 orange	1.00
Maria Alcala	do	4 avocados and 3 guavas	1.00
Mrs. Moses Casas	do	15 apples and 1 plant	1.00
Domingo Mato	do	2 guavas	1.00
Victoria Panique	do	3 avocado seeds	1.00
Josephine Ramos	do	2 guavas	1.00
Pablo Torres	do	11 apples	1.00
Consumsion Munoz	do	13 red haws	1.00
Frieda Pickens	do	5 tangerines, 2 stalks sugarcane, and 2 plants.	1.00
I. Rudelnick	do	1 orange	1.00
Alberto M. Cabanas	do	3 oranges	1.00
Paulino Lucio	do	3 guavas	1.00
W. M. Hunt	do	1 orange	1.00
Alberto Gonzalez	do	16 tangerines, 2 grapefruit, and 2 oranges.	2.00
Maria T. Elonday	do	4 oranges	1.00
Domitila Rosillo Ayala	do	75 guavas	2.00
William L. Berry	do	Orchid plants	31.25
Mrs. Antonio Esponosa	do	13 guavas	1.00
Alfonso Navarro	do	2 guavas	1.00
Manuel Solis	do	do	1.00
Dolores Rodarte	do	10 avocados	1.00
Teresa Victoria	do	2 avocados	1.00
Mrs. G. G. Carter	do	1 avocado, 2 cherimoyas, and 4 grapefruit.	1.00
Juana H. Herrera	do	8 apples	1.00
Antonio Trevino	do	5 plants	1.00
Jose Vega	do	2 avocados	1.00
M. L. Vela	do	6 oranges	1.00
L. A. Mitchell	do	7 avocados	1.00
Mrs. Carmen G. Elisa	do	48 avocados	2.00
Sarate Ratcliff	do	3 guavas and 5 plants	1.00
Lupe Dennis	do	2 guavas	1.00
Eloise Ratcliff	do	4 plants	1.00
Na Agruirre Silter	do	2 apples	1.00
Pablo Gonzales	do	1 guava	1.00
Jim Alonzo	do	9 avocados	1.00
Victor Beltram	do	6 avocado seed	1.00
Judge Penn	do	63 apples	1.00
Eloy Garcia	do	4 avocados	1.00
Enrique Valdez	do	4 guavas	1.00
Arthur Vela	do	1 papaya	1.00
Elena Bosque	do	7 apples	1.00
Henrique Aranda	do	8 limes	1.00
J. G. Guajardo	do	2 oranges	1.00
Rosendo Rodrigues	do	1 guava	1.00
Mrs. Petra Chacon	do	30 apples, 3 avocados, and 5 plants.	1.50
Mrs. Carlote Duarte	do	6 plants	1.00
D. C. Nester	do	14 oranges	1.00
Juana Hernandez	do	1 guava	1.00
M. A. Garza	do	5 bulbs and 5 cuttings	1.00

LIST OF CURRENT QUARANTINE AND OTHER RESTRICTIVE ORDERS AND MISCELLANEOUS REGULATIONS

[The domestic and foreign quarantine and other restrictive orders summarized herein, are issued under the authority of the Plant Quarantine Act of Aug. 20, 1912, as amended. The Mexican border regulations and the export-certification regulations are issued under specific acts of Congress.]

QUARANTINE ORDERS

The numbers assigned to these quarantines indicate merely the chronological order of issuance of both domestic and foreign quarantines in one numerical series. The quarantine numbers missing in this list are quarantines which have either been superseded or revoked. For convenience of reference these quarantines are here classified as domestic and foreign, the domestic quarantines being divided into (1) those applying primarily to the continental United States and (2) those applying primarily to shipments from and to the Territories of Hawaii and Puerto Rico.

DOMESTIC PLANT QUARANTINES

QUARANTINES APPLYING TO THE CONTINENTAL UNITED STATES

Black stem rust.—Quarantine No. 38, revised, effective September 1, 1937: Prohibits, except as provided in the rules and regulations supplemental thereto, effective August 1, 1931, the movement into any of the protected States, namely, Colorado, Illinois, Indiana, Iowa, Michigan, Minnesota, Missouri, Montana, Nebraska, North Dakota, Ohio, Pennsylvania, South Dakota, Virginia, West Virginia, Wisconsin, and Wyoming, as well as the movement from any one of said protected States into any other protected State of the common barberry (*Berberis vulgaris*), or other species of *Berberis* or *Mahonia* or parts thereof capable of propagation, on account of the black stem rust of grains. The regulations place no restrictions on the interstate movement of Japanese barberry (*B. thunbergii*) or any of its rust-resistant varieties, or of cuttings (without roots) of *Mahonia* shipped for decorative purposes and not for propagation.

Gypsy moth and brown-tail moth.—Quarantine No. 45, revised, effective November 4, 1935: Prohibits, except as provided in the rules and regulations supplemental thereto, revised, effective November 4, 1935, the movement interstate to any point outside of the infested area, or from points in the generally infested area to points in the lightly infested area, of stone or quarry products, and of the plants and the plant products listed therein. The quarantine covers Rhode Island and parts of the States of Connecticut, Maine, Massachusetts, New Hampshire, and Vermont.

Japanese beetle.—Quarantine No. 48, revised, effective March 1, 1937: Prohibits, except as provided in the rules and regulations supplemental thereto, revised, effective March 1, 1937, as amended effective May 10, 1937, the interstate movement of (1) fruits and vegetables; (2) nursery, ornamental, and greenhouse stock and other plants; and (3) sand, soil, earth, peat, compost, and manure, from the quarantined area to or through any point outside thereof. The quarantined area includes the entire States of Massachusetts, Rhode Island, Connecticut, New Jersey, and Delaware, and the District of Columbia, and portions of the States of Maine, New Hampshire, Vermont, New York, Pennsylvania, Maryland, Virginia, West Virginia, and Ohio.

Pink bollworm.—Quarantine No. 52, revised, effective October 14, 1936: Prohibits, except as provided in the rules and regulations supplemental thereto, revised effective October 14, 1936, as amended, effective January 3, 1938, the interstate movement from the regulated areas of Texas, New Mexico, and Arizona, of (1) cotton, wild cotton, including all parts of either cotton or wild cotton plants, seed cotton, cotton lint, linters, and all other forms of unmanufactured cotton fiber, gin waste, cottonseed, cottonseed hulls, and cottonseed cake and meal; (2) bagging and other containers and wrappers of cotton and cotton products; (3) railway cars, boats, and other vehicles which have been used in conveying cotton or cotton products or which are fouled with such products; (4) hay and other farm products; and (5) farm household goods, farm equipment, and, if contaminated with cotton, any other articles.

Thurberia weevil.—Quarantine No. 61, revised, effective August 1, 1927: Prohibits the interstate movement of *Thurberia*, including all parts of the plant, from any point in Arizona and prohibits, except as provided in the rules and regulations supplemental thereto effective October 2, 1933, as amended effective October 22, 1936, the interstate movement from the regulated area of Arizona of (1) cotton, including all parts of the plant, seed cotton, cotton lint, linters, and all other forms of unmanufactured cotton lint, gin waste, cottonseed, cottonseed hulls, and cottonseed cake and meal; (2) bagging and other containers and wrappers of cotton and cotton products; (3) railway cars, boats, and other vehicles which have been used in conveying cotton and cotton products, or which are fouled with such products; (4) hay and other farm products; and (5) farm household goods, farm equipment, and, if contaminated with cotton, any other articles.

White-pine blister rust.—Quarantine No. 63, effective October 1, 1926: Prohibits, except as provided in the rules and regulations supplemental thereto, revised effective March 1, 1937, the interstate movement from every State in the continental United States and the District of Columbia of five-leafed pines (*Pinus*) or currant and gooseberry plants (*Ribes* and *Grossularia*), including cultivated or wild or ornamental sorts.

Mexican fruitfly.—Quarantine No. 64, effective October 15, 1937: Prohibits, except as provided in the rules and regulations supplemental thereto, revised effective October 15, 1937, the interstate movement from the regulated area of Texas of fruits of all varieties.

Woodgate rust.—Quarantine No. 65, effective November 1, 1928: Prohibits, except as provided in the rules and regulations supplemental thereto, effective November 1, 1928, as amended, effective April 1, 1929, the interstate movement from the regulated area in the State of New York of trees, branches, limbs, or twigs of Scotch pine (*Pinus sylvestris*), Canary Island pine (*P. canariensis*), slash pine (*P. caribaea*), Japanese red pine (*P. densiflora*), Corsican pine (*P. nigra poiretiana*), stone pine (*P. pinea*), western yellow pine (*P. ponderosa*), Monterey pine (*P. radiata*), loblolly pine (*P. taeda*), or Jersey pine (*P. virginiana*), or of any variety thereof, or of any species or variety of hard pine hereafter found to be susceptible to the Woodgate rust.

Dutch elm disease.—Quarantine No. 71, effective February 25, 1935: Prohibits, except as provided in the rules and regulations supplemental thereto, effective February 25, 1935, as amended effective November 9, 1937, the interstate movement from the regulated areas in the States of New Jersey, New York, and Connecticut to or through any point outside thereof, of elm plants or parts thereof of all species of the genus *Ulmus*, irrespective of whether nursery, forest, or privately grown, including (1) trees, plants, leaves, twigs, branches, bark, roots, trunks, cuttings, and scions of such plants; (2) logs or cordwood of such plants; and (3) lumber, crates, boxes, barrels, packing cases, and other containers manufactured in whole or in part from such plants, unless the wood is entirely free from bark.

QUARANTINES APPLYING TO THE TERRITORIES OF HAWAII AND PUERTO RICO

Hawaiian fruits and vegetables.—Quarantine No. 13, revised, effective June 1, 1917: Prohibits, except as provided in the rules and regulations supplemental thereto, revised, effective June 1, 1930, the movement from the Territory of Hawaii into or through any other Territory, State, or District of the United States, of all fruits and vegetables in the natural or raw state, on account of the Mediterranean fruitfly (*Ceratitis capitata*) and the melonfly (*Dacus cucurbitae*).

Sugarcane.—Quarantine No. 16, revised, effective January 1, 1935: Prohibits the movement from the Territories of Hawaii and Puerto Rico into or through any other Territory, State, or District of the United States of canes of sugarcane, or cuttings or parts thereof, sugarcane leaves, and bagasse, on account of certain injurious insects and diseases, except that movement will be allowed under permit of specific materials on condition that they have been or are to be so treated, processed, or manufactured that, in the judgment of the Department, their movement will involve no pest risk.

Sweetpotato.—Quarantine No. 30, revised, effective October 10, 1934: Prohibits the movement from the Territories of Hawaii and Puerto Rico into or through any other Territory, State, or District of the United States of any variety of sweetpotato (*Ipomoea batatas* Poir.), regardless of the use for which the same is intended, on account of the sweetpotato stem borer (*Omphisa anastomosalis* Guen.) and the sweetpotato scarabee (*Euscepes batatae* Waterh.).

Banana plants.—Quarantine No. 32, effective April 1, 1918: Prohibits the movement from the Territories of Hawaii and Puerto Rico into or through any other Territory, State, or District of the United States of any species or variety of banana plants (*Musa* spp.), regardless of the use for which the same is intended, on account of two injurious weevils (*Rhabdocnemis obscurus* and *Metamasius hemipterus*).

Hawaiian and Puerto Rican cotton, cottonseed, and cottonseed products.— Quarantine No. 47, effective August 15, 1920: Prohibits, except as provided in the rules and regulations supplemental thereto, effective August 15, 1920, the movement of cotton, cottonseed, and cottonseed products, except oil, from the Territories of Hawaii and Puerto Rico into or through any other Territory, State, or District of the United States on account of the pink bollworm (*Pectinophora gossypiella* Saund.) and the cotton-blister mite (*Eriophyes gossypii* Banks), respectively.

United States quarantined to protect Hawaii.—Quarantine No. 51, effective October 1, 1921: Prohibits, except as provided in the rules and regulations supplemental thereto, effective October 1, 1921, the movement from the United States to the Territory of Hawaii, as ships' stores or as baggage or effects of passengers or crews, of sugarcane, corn (other than shelled corn), cotton, alfalfa, and the fruits of the avocado and papaya in the natural or raw state, on account of injurious insects, especially the sugarcane borer (*Diatraea saccharalis* Fab.), the alfalfa weevil (*Hypera postica* Gyll.), the cotton boll weevil (*Anthonomus grandis* Boh.), the papaya fruitfly (*Toxotrypana curvicauda* Gerst.), and certain insect enemies of the fruit of the avocado.

Puerto Rican fruits and vegetables.—Quarantine No. 58, effective July 1, 1925: Prohibits, except as provided in the rules and regulations supplemental thereto, effective July 1, 1925, as amended effective January 1, 1933, the movement from the Territory of Puerto Rico into or through any other Territory, State, or District of the United States of all fruits and vegetables in the raw or unprocessed state, on account of injurious insects, including the West Indian fruitfly (*Anastrepha fraterculus* Wied.), and the bean-pod borer (*Maruca testulalis* Geyer).

Sand, soil, or earth, with plants from Hawaii and Puerto Rico.—Quarantine No. 60, revised, effective September 1, 1936: Prohibits the movement from the Territories of Hawaii and Puerto Rico into or through any other Territory, State, or District of the United States of sand (other than clean ocean sand), soil, or earth around the roots of plants, to prevent the spread of white grubs, the Japanese rose beetle, and termites or white ants. Provision is made for the retention of potted plants on board vessels from Hawaii and Puerto Rico when evidence is presented satisfactory to the plant quarantine inspector that the soil has been so treated, or is so safeguarded, as to eliminate pest risk.

FOREIGN PLANT QUARANTINES

Pink bollworm.—Quarantine No. 8, effective July 1, 1913, with revised regulations effective July 1, 1917: Forbids the importation from any foreign locality and country, excepting only the locality of the Imperial Valley in the State of Baja California, Mexico, of cottonseed (including seed cotton) of all species and varieties and cottonseed hulls. Seed cotton, cottonseed, and cottonseed hulls from the Imperial Valley may be entered under permit and regulation.

Seeds of avocado or alligator pear.—Quarantine No. 12, effective February 27, 1914: Forbids the importation from Mexico and the countries of Central America of the seed of the avocado or alligator pear on account of the avocado weevil (*Heilipus lauri*).

Sugarcane.—Quarantine No. 15, revised, effective October 1, 1934: Prohibits the importation from all foreign countries and localities of canes of sugarcane, or cuttings or parts thereof, sugarcane leaves, and bagasse, on account of certain injurious insects and diseases, except that importation will be allowed under permit of specific materials on condition that they have been or are to be so treated, processed, or manufactured that, in the judgment of the Department, their entry will involve no pest risk.

Citrus nursery stock.—Quarantine No. 19, revised, effective September 1, 1934: Forbids the importation from all foreign localities and countries of all citrus nursery stock, including buds and scions, on account of the citrus canker and other dangerous citrus diseases. The term "citrus," as used in this quarantine, includes all plants belonging to the tribe Citrinae.

Indian corn or maize and related plants.—Quarantine No. 24, effective July 1, 1916, as amended effective April 1, 1917, and April 23, 1917: Forbids the importation from southeastern Asia (including India, Siam, Indo-China, and China),

Malayan Archipelago, Australia, New Zealand, Oceania, Philippine Islands, Taiwan (Formosa), Japan, and adjacent islands, in the raw or unmanufactured state, of seed and all other portions of Indian corn or maize (*Zea mays* L.) and the closely related plants, including all species of Teosinte (*Euchlaena*), jobs-tears (*Coix*), Polytoca, Chionachne, and Sclerachne, on account of the downy mildews and Physoderma diseases of Indian corn, except that Indian corn or maize may be imported under permit and upon compliance with the conditions prescribed in the regulations of the Secretary of Agriculture.

Citrus fruits.—Quarantine No. 28, effective August 1, 1917: Forbids the importation from eastern and southeastern Asia (including India, Siam, Indo-China, and China), the Malayan Archipelago, the Philippine Islands, Oceania (except Australia, Tasmania, and New Zealand), Japan (including Taiwan (Formosa) and other islands adjacent to Japan), and the Union of South Africa, of all species and varieties of citrus fruits, on account of the citrus canker, except that oranges of the mandarin class (including satsuma and tangerine varieties) may be imported under permit and upon compliance with the conditions prescribed in the regulations of the Secretary of Agriculture.

Sweetpotato and yam.—Quarantine No. 29, effective January 1, 1918: Forbids the importation for any purpose of any variety of sweetpotatoes and yams (*Ipomoea batatas* and *Dioscorea* spp.), from all foreign countries and localities, on account of the sweetpotato weevils (*Cylas* spp.) and the sweetpotato scarabee (*Euscepes batatae*).

Banana plants.—Quarantine No. 31, effective April 1, 1918: Forbids the importation for any purpose of any species or variety of banana plants (*Musa* spp.), or portions thereof, from all foreign countries and localities, on account of the banana-root borer (*Cosmopolites sordidus*). This quarantine places no restrictions on the importation of the fruit of the banana. (For restrictions on the entry of the fruit of the banana see quarantine 56.)

Bamboo.—Quarantine No. 34, effective October 1, 1918: Forbids the importation for any purpose of any variety of bamboo seeds, plants, or cuttings thereof capable of propagation, including all genera and species of the tribe Bambuseae, from all foreign countries and localities, on account of dangerous plant diseases, including the bamboo smut (*Ustilago shiraiana*). This quarantine order does not apply to bamboo timber consisting of the mature dried culms or canes which are imported for fishing rods, furniture making, or other purposes, or to any kind of articles manufactured from bamboo, or to bamboo shoots cooked or otherwise preserved.

Nursery stock, plants, and seeds.—Quarantine No. 37, effective June 1, 1919: Forbids, except as provided in the rules and regulations supplemental thereto, revised effective December 22, 1930, and amended effective January 14, 1935, the importation of seeds, nursery stock, and other plants and plant products capable of propagation from all foreign countries and localities on account of certain injurious insects and fungous diseases. Under this quarantine the following plant products may be imported without restriction when free from sand, soil, or earth, unless covered by special quarantine or other restrictive orders: Plant products imported for medicinal, food, or manufacturing purposes, and field, vegetable, and flower seeds, except seeds of *Lathyrus* and *Vicia*. Cut flowers from the Dominion of Canada are also allowed entry without permit. The entry of the following nursery stock and other plants and seeds is permitted under permit:

Under regulation 3:

(1) Bulbs, corms, or root stocks (pips) of the following genera: *Lilium* (lily), *Convallaria* (lily-of-the-valley), *Hyacinthus* (hyacinth), *Tulipa* (tulip), and *Crocus;* and, until further notice, *Chionodoxa* (glory-of-the-snow), *Galanthus* (snowdrop), *Scilla* (squill), *Fritillaria*, *Muscari* (grape-hyacinth), *Ixia*, and *Eranthis* (winter aconite); and *Narcissus* (daffodil and jonquil).

(2) Cuttings, scions, and buds of fruits or nuts: *Provided*, That cuttings, scions, and buds of fruits or nuts may be imported from Asia, Japan, Philippine Islands, and Oceania (including Australia and New Zealand) under the provisions of regulation 14 only. (Stocks of fruits or nuts may not be imported, under permit or otherwise.)

(3) Rose stocks, including Manetti, *Rosa multiflora* (brier rose), and *R. rugosa*.

(4) Nuts, including palm seeds for growing purposes: *Provided*, That such nuts or seeds shall be free from pulp.

(5) Seeds of fruit, forest, ornamental, and shade trees, seeds of deciduous and evergreen ornamental shrubs, and seeds of hardy perennial plants: *Provided*, That such seeds shall be free from pulp: *Provided further*, That citrus seeds may be imported only through specified ports subject to disinfection as provided in regulation 9: *Provided further*, That mango seeds may not be imported under-permit or otherwise, except from the countries of North America, Central America, and South America, and the West Indies.

Importations from countries not maintaining inspection of nursery stock, other plants and parts of plants, including seeds, the entry of which is permissible under this regulation, may be made under permit upon compliance with these regulations in limited quantities for public-service purposes only, but this limitation shall not apply to tree seeds.

(6) Materials permitted entry under Quarantine No. 56 for consumption purposes are authorized entry under this regulation for propagation.

Under regulation 14: Provision exists in this regulation for the entry of most kinds of plants that are not covered by other regulations of this quarantine or by other quarantines.

Under regulation 15: Provision exists for the entry in unlimited quantities of most kinds of plants which can be considered as peculiar to or standard productions of the Dominion of Canada, as opposed to stock imported into the Dominion from foreign countries and held or grown on there for later sale.

European corn borer.—Quarantine No. 41, revised, effective June 1, 1926; Forbids, except as provided in the rules and regulations supplemental thereto, revised effective March 1, 1933, the importation from all foreign countries and localities of the stalk and all other parts, whether used for packing or other purposes, in the raw or unmanufactured state, of Indian corn or maize, broomcorn, sweet sorghums, grain sorghums, Sudan grass, Johnson grass, sugarcane, pearl millet, napier grass, teosinte, and jobs-tears, on account of the European corn borer (*Pyrausta nubilalis*) and other dangerous insects and plant diseases.

Rice.—Quarantine No. 55, revised, effective November 23, 1933: Forbids the importation of seed or paddy rice from all foreign countries and localities except the Republic of Mexico, and forbids the importation of rice straw and rice hulls from all foreign countries and localities, and seed or paddy rice from the Republic of Mexico, except as provided in the rules and regulations supplemental thereto, effective July 1, 1933, as amended effective August 1, 1934, on account of injurious fungous diseases of rice, including downy mildew (*Sclerospora macrocarpa*), leaf smut (*Entyloma oryzae*), blight (*Oospora oryztorum*), and glume blotch (*Melanomma glumarum*), as well as dangerous insect pests.

Fruits and vegetables.—Quarantine No. 56, effective November 1, 1923: Forbids, except as provided in the rules and regulations supplemental thereto, revised, effective December 1, 1936, the importation of fruits and vegetables, except as restricted, as to certain countries and districts, by special quarantines and other orders, and of plants or portions of plants used as packing material in connection with shipments of such fruits and vegetables from all foreign countries and localities other than the Dominion of Canada, on account of injurious insects, including fruit and melon flies (Trypetidae). Includes and supersedes Quarantine No. 49 on account of the citrus blackfly.

Flag smut.—Quarantine No. 59, effective February 1, 1926: Forbids the importation of all species and varieties of wheat (*Triticum* spp.) and wheat products, unless so milled or so processed as to have destroyed all flag-smut spores, from India, Japan, China, Australia, Union of South Africa, Italy, and Spain.

Packing materials.—Quarantine No. 69, effective July 1, 1933, as amended, effective July 1, 1933: Forbids the entry from all foreign countries and localities of the following materials when used as packing for other commodities, except in special cases where preparation, processing, or manufacture are judged by an inspector of the United States Department of Agriculture to have eliminated risk of carrying injurious insects and plant diseases: Rice straw, hulls, and chaff; cotton and cotton products: sugarcane, including bagasse; bamboo leaves and small shoots; leaves of plants; forest litter; and soil with an appreciable admixture of vegetable matter not therein provided for by regulation. All parts of corn and allied plants are likewise prohibited except from Mexico and the countries of Central America, the West Indies, and South America. This quarantine also brings under restriction, involving inspection at will by the Department but requiring no permit or certificate, the following when used as packing: Cereal straw, chaff, and hulls (other than rice); corn and allied plants from Mexico, Central America, the West Indies, and South America; willow twigs from Europe; grasses, hay, and similar plant mixtures from all countries; and authorized soil packing materials from all countries. This quarantine does not cover such widely used packing materials as excelsior, paper, sawdust, ground cork, charcoal, and various other materials.

Dutch elm disease.— Quarantine No. 70, revised, effective January 1, 1935: Forbids the importation from Europe, on account of a disease due to the fungus *Graphium ulmi*, of seeds, leaves, plants, cuttings, and scions of elm or related plants, defined to include all genera of the family Ulmaceae; logs of elm and related plants; lumber, timber, or veneer of such plants if bark is present on them; and crates, boxes, barrels, packing cases, and other containers, and other articles manufactured in whole or in part from the wood of elm or related plants if not free from bark.

OTHER RESTRICTIVE ORDERS

The regulation of the entry of nursery stock from foreign countries into the United States was specifically provided for in the Plant Quarantine Act. The act further provides for the similar regulation of any other class of plants or plant products when the need therefor shall be determined. The entry of the plants and plant products listed below has been brought under such regulation.

Nursery stock.—The conditions governing the entry of nursery stock and other plants and seeds from all foreign countries and localities are indicated above under "Foreign plant quarantines." (See Quarantine No. 37, revised.)

Potatoes.—The order of December 22, 1913, and the regulations issued thereunder, revised, effective March 1, 1922, and amended, effective December 1, 1936, restrict the importation of potatoes from all foreign countries and localities except the Dominion of Canada and Bermuda, on account of injurious potato diseases and insect pests. The importation of potatoes is now authorized from Bermuda, Canada, Cuba, the Dominican Republic, Estonia, Latvia, Spain (including the Canary Islands), and the States of Chihuahua and Sonora, and the northern territory of Baja California, Mexico.

Cotton and cotton wrappings.—The order of April 27, 1915, and the rules and regulations issued thereunder, revised, effective February 24, 1923, amended effective May 1, 1924, December 15, 1924, and December 11, 1937, restrict the importation of cotton and cotton wrappings from all foreign countries and localities, on account of injurious insects, including the pink bollworm.

Cottonseed products.—The two orders of June 23, 1917, and the rules and regulations issued thereunder, effective July 16, 1917, amended, effective August 7, 1925, restrict the importation of cottonseed cake and meal and all other cottonseed products except oil from all foreign countries and localities, and the importation of cottonseed oil from Mexico, on account of injurious insects, including the pink bollworm: *Provided,* That these commodities which originate in, and are shipped directly from, the Imperial Valley, Baja California, Mexico, may enter without restriction.

Plant safeguard regulations.—These rules and regulations, revised, effective December 1, 1932, provide safeguards for the landing or unloading for transshipment and exportation and for transportation and exportation in bond of restricted or prohibited plants and plant products when it is determined that such entry can be made without involving risk to the plant cultures of the United States, and also provide for the safeguarding of such plant material at a port or within the territorial limits of the United States where entry or landing is not intended or where entry has been refused.

Rules and regulations governing the movement of plants and plant products into and out of the District of Columbia.—These rules and regulations, revised effective April 30, 1931, are promulgated under the amendment to the Plant Quarantine Act of May 31, 1920. They provide for the regulation of the movement of plants and plant products, including nursery stock, from or into the District of Columbia and for the control of injurious plant diseases and insect pests within the said District.

MISCELLANEOUS REGULATIONS

Rules and regulations prohibiting the movement of cotton and cottonseed from Mexico into the United States and governing the entry into the United States of railway cars and other vehicles, freight, express, baggage, or other materials from Mexico at border points.—These rules and regulations, promulgated June 23, 1917, pursuant to authority given in the appropriation act for the United States Department of Agriculture for the fiscal year 1918, and since repeated annually, and amended effective January 29, 1920, are designed to prevent the entry of the pink bollworm of cotton which is known to exist widely in Mexico. They provide for the examination of passengers' baggage, for the disinfection of railway cars, freight, express, and other shipments, and for the cleaning of domestic cars handling Mexican freight. All fees collected for disinfecting railway cars are deposited in the United States Treasury as miscellaneous receipts.

The inspectors concerned in the enforcement of these regulations at border points are charged also with enforcement of restrictions on the entry of plants and plant products under various foreign plant quarantines.

Regulations governing sanitary export certification.—These regulations, revised effective September 21, 1936, were promulgated pursuant to authority granted in the Agricultural Appropriation Act of May 17, 1935 (49 Stat. 268), and repeated in subsequent appropriation acts. They provide for the inspection and certification of domestic plants and plant products intended for export to countries requiring such certification. All fees collected for this service are deposited in the United States Treasury as miscellaneous receipts.

ORGANIZATION OF THE BUREAU OF ENTOMOLOGY AND PLANT QUARANTINE

LEE A. STRONG, *Chief.*
S. A. ROHWER, *Assistant Chief.*
AVERY S. HOYT, *Assistant Chief.*
P. N. ANNAND, *Special Research Assistant.*
F. H. SPENCER, *Business Manager.*
ROLLA P. CURRIE, *Editor.*
MABEL COLCORD, *Librarian.*
J. A. HYSLOP, *in Charge, Division of Insect Pest Survey and Information.*
J. I. HAMBLETON, *in Charge, Division of Bee Culture Investigations.*
D. L. VAN DINE, *in Charge, Division of Fruit Insect Investigations.*
F. C. CRAIGHEAD, *in Charge, Division of Forest Insect Investigations.*
W. H. WHITE, *in Charge, Division of Truck Crop and Garden Insect Investigations.*
C. M. PACKARD, *in Charge, Division of Cereal and Forage Insect Investigations.*
R. W. HARNED, *in Charge, Division of Cotton Insect Investigations.*
F. C. BISHOPP, *in Charge, Division of Insects Affecting Man and Animals.*
L. A. HAWKINS, *in Charge, Division of Control Investigations.*
R. C. ROARK, *in Charge, Division of Insecticides and Fungicides.*
C. F. W. MUESEBECK, *in Charge, Division of Insect Identification.*
C. P. CLAUSEN, *in Charge, Division of Foreign Parasite Introduction.*
S. B. FRACKER, *in Charge, Division of Plant Disease Control.*
B. M. GADDIS, *in Charge, Division of Domestic Plant Quarantines.*
E. R. SASSCER, *in Charge, Division of Foreign Plant Quarantines.*
A. F. BURGESS, *in Field Charge, Gypsy Moth and Brown-Tail Moth Control* (headquarters, *Greenfield, Mass.*).
E. G. BREWER, *in Field Charge, Japanese Beetle and Gypsy Moth and Brown-Tail Moth Quarantines, European Corn Borer Certification, and Dutch Elm Disease Eradication* (headquarters, *Bloomfield, N. J.*).
R. E. MCDONALD, *in Field Charge, Pink Bollworm and Thurberia Weevil Quarantines* (headquarters, *San Antonio, Tex.*).
P. A. HOIDALE, *in Field Charge, Mexican Fruitfly Quarantine* (headquarters, *Harlingen, Tex.*).
A. C. BAKER, *in Field Charge, Fruitfly Investigations* (headquarters, *Mexico City, Mexico*).
W. E. DOVE, *in Field Charge, Screwworm Control* (headquarters, *San Antonio, Tex.*).

318